SLOW FOOD ALMANAC

ALMANAC OF THE INTERNATIONAL
SLOW FOOD MOVEMENT

Publishing director
Carlo Petrini

Editor
Monica Mascarino

Assistant editors
Francesco Bertello, Simona Luparia

Photo research editor
Chiara Cauda

Editor of the Italian edition
Silvia Ceriani

Editor of the English edition
John Irving

Editor of the German edition
Ulrich Rosenbaum

Editor of the French edition
Eric Chenebier

Editor of the Spanish edition
Juan Bureo

Editors of the Portuguese edition
Roberta Marins de Sá, Karla Queiroz
de Melo

Editor of the Russian edition
Igor Danilov, Lilia Smelkova

Editor of the Japanese edition
Toshiya Yoshikai

Coordination
Mavi Negro, Gigi Piumatti

Translations
Luisa Balacco, Svetlana Berezovskaya,
Simona Caldera, Giulia Fabioux,
Valentina García, Elena Giovanelli,
Ryouji Ikarashi, Pierre Le Chevallier,
Debra Levine, Catherine Mas, Fanny
Meroni, Emanuela Miretti, Davide
Panzieri, Carla Ranicki, Ronnie Richards,
Jennifer Robson, Marisol Rodríguez
Val, Julia Rommel, Annette Seimer,
Victoria Smelkova, Svetlana Stigneeva,
Doris Wiesbauer, Winnie Yang

Illustrations
Marco Cazzato - www.marcocazzato.it

Art director and layout
Stefano Pallaro

Photo-offset lithography
Imago, Marene (Cn)

Printed by
Rotolito Lombarda, Pioltello (Mi)

ISBN ALMANACCO 2008
978 88 8499 182 9

Cover
Chichicastenango, Guatemala,
Tibor Bognár, Corbis

Issue closed
3/09/2008

Slow Food Editore srl
Via della Mendicità Istruita, 45
12042 Bra (Cn) Italy
tel +39 0172 419611
fax +39 0172 411218
almanac@slowfood.com
www.slowfood.com

Administration
via Vittorio Emanuele II, 248
12042 Bra (Cn) Italy
tel +39 0172 419611
fax +39 0172 421293

Advertising
Slow Food Promozione srl
Ivan Piasentin, Enrico Bonura,
Gabriele Cena, Erika Margiaria
via Vittorio Emanuele II, 248
12042 Bra (Cn) Italy
tel. 0172 419611
fax 0172 413640
promozione@slowfood.it

The publisher is prepared to recognize
the claims of copyright holders where
prior contact was impossible.

Mixed Sources
Product group from well-managed
forests and other controlled sources
www.fsc.org Cert no. SW-COC-002295
© 1996 Forest Stewardship Council

SLOW FOOD
NETWORK
BIODIVERSITY
LOCAL ECONOMY
PLEASURE
TRADITION

THE FLOW
OF WORDS

The year we describe here does not follow the rhythm of the days or the passing of the months or the succession of the seasons. The year we speak of has a flow of its own. Of insights and observations, of the actions that give life to the Slow Food galaxy.

And also of words, five words. Network, biodiversity, local economy, pleasure, tradition. You find them here in theoretical reflections—philosophical, economic, scientific—in accounts of real-life events and stories of specific projects. They are spoken by people who play an active part in the Slow Food association, and have done for years, and people who support it with their own authoritative contribution of ideas and competences.

Our five words clash with the three letters of an acronym: OGM, Genetically Modified Organisms. The battle against transgenic crops and foods is one of the ambits to which the Slow Food devotes most political and civil commitment. Here it is addressed through national analyses which, read together, evidence contradictions and dangers, expose logics and interests and unmask rhetoric. As evidence is backed up by data, so perplexities turn to protest.

Network, biodiversity, local economy, pleasure and tradition.

Five words that are also stifled. In the cries of alarm of those who denounce the emergencies of the planet and the world of food: rights denied, the devastating effects of globalization, the market economy at local level.

The pages of this book conclude on these *thoughts*.

The *words*, instead, continue to be spoken.

CONTENTS

EDITORIALS   7

*Εno-Εco-Neo. A Story
in Three Acts*
John Irving   22

NETWORK

Balancing Act
Michael Dimock   28

Sustainable Communities
Fritjof Capra   36

Brotherhood
Samuel Karanja Muhunyu   42

Learning Together
Cristina Bertazzoni   48

Leaving A Mark
Elizabeth Manning   54

BIODIVERSITY

Domestic and Wild
Piero Sardo   58

Food Sovereignty
Pat Roy Mooney   66

The Right Recipe
Serena Milano   74

Aromas in a global world
Mariana Guimarães Weiler   80

Ketchup Isn't A Vegetable
Manfred Flieser   86

LOCAL ECONOMY

The Arda Valley
Dessislava Dimitrova   92

The Alternative
Gianluca Brunori   100

Souk Every Monday
Rami Zurayk   108

The Yale Generation
Joshua Viertel   114

The Taste for Health
Andrea Pezzana   120

PLEASURE

Epicurus docet
Alberto Capatti   126

The Music of the Spheres
Nicolas Joly   134

I Drink Alone
Michel Smith   140

Eating Up Culture
Matthew Fort   146

Three bees for a spoonful of honey
Narita Shigeyuki   152

TRADITION

No job for archeologists
José N. Iturriaga de la Fuente   156

Pesach Dinner
Moshe Basson   164

Flavor in Music
Kennet Erwin Konesni   168

Scrapbook
Lilia Zaouali   174

Flour House
Margarida Nogueira   180

FOCUS GMO

Innovative Genomes, Old Arguments
Luca Colombo   184

South American Harvest
Miguel A. Altieri   188

The World's Breadbasket
Maria Teresa Morresi   192

Thus Spoke Percy
Pamela Cuthbert   196

The figures don't add up
Vandana Shiva   200

The Debate in Australia
Richard Cornish   204

When Two Elephants Fight
Madieng Seck   208

The Battle in Catalonia
Francesc Balañá   212

UK Doubts
Joanna Blythman   216

Insecurity and Death
Alexander Baranov   220

GLOBAL/LOCAL

New Creative Spaces
George Ritzer   224

The dream we need
Serge Latouche   228

Zero Waste
Robin Murray   232

Food is Sharing
Aminata D. Traorè   238

Rural Poor
Tewolde Berhan Gebre Egziabher   240

APPENDIX   244

☺ Carlo Petrini

President Slow Food International

It is often necessary to interpret major changes not just in terms of their immediate repercussions on our daily lives but also with an eye to the future. Not that I wish to sound immodest but I do believe that, as you read these words, you are experiencing such a change. As a Slow Food member, you are about to browse through the first historic number of our new publication, the *Slow Food Almanac*. The *Almanac* is a milestone in the history of a movement that has become a unique melting pot of diversity. The strength of Slow Food has increasingly shifted from what it gives its members to what its members can give to it, to its intellectual growth and to the perception it generates of itself externally—and when I say externally I mean the whole world.

As we reap the rewards of Terra Madre among food producers worldwide, we are seeing for ourselves how the topics we address and the work we do are so universal that they appeal to any type of human diversity. Food respectful of memory, culture, people and the planet we live on is an ancestral element, a sacred part of our existence that interweaves our experiences and those of nature. It is a means of self-expression, a way of getting on with mutual respect. More than anything else, food truly is what we are—irrespective of the differences that mark our identities. Today, restoring food—debased along with its overseers, exploited as a tool of control and global power—to its central role in our passage though the world is an act of great political relevance. To some extent, it is a revolutionary act.

Think of what Slow Food is today, think of the people it is made up of: food producers from every corner of the planet (who we should learn to embrace and involve more and more) and all sorts of people who either know or want to know what they are eating—for their own pleasure, for their own health, for the health of their children, for a better world to come. We are a representation of diversity in miniature. Within Slow Food peasants in the most isolated rural regions team up with hard-bitten city dwellers keen to rediscover slowness as a homeopathic cure, their lives increasingly disoriented by modern complexity and the speed on which it gorges itself.

Yet it is precisely in the complexity that we somehow represent so well that we have to find the creative flair and the force to make our demands for better, cleaner and fairer food heard. We must fear the disorder that surrounds us no longer. Precisely the commitment to keep an association as complex as post-Terra Madre Slow Food united has made us realize that we have to put our faith in that disorder. We only need to decide what type of life we want to live and how we want to live it to realize that complexity can bear glorious fruits. This is the lesson we learn from nature and biodiversity, this is the lesson we learn from the pathetic failures of all those who have sought to find an easy way out of complexity and disorder with a barrage of fast food chains, GMOs and intercontinental transport, filling up supermarket shelves and making them identical everywhere with no respect whatsoever for the seasons and the diversity of peoples. The more we grow as an association, the more we will be disorderly. The more we welcome new friends from faraway places, the more we will learn to live in the world. This *Almanac* cannot represent everybody, but it is our principal point of contact and it does provide a space for us to get to know and talk to each other and understand how this chaotic complexity of ours can improve our lives and even please Mother Earth herself. Yes, because we also defend the right to pleasure of the planet we live on.

John Kariuki Mwangi

Vice-President Slow Food International

With poverty continuing to encourage rural-urban migration across the developing world and the average age of farmers reaching all-time highs in many countries, one of our greatest challenges for the future is to support young people who wish to enter or carry on working in farming and food production. In poorer nations, the promise of the city often disappoints, leading to social and cultural disintegration and further erosion of unique food heritages and identities. Simultaneously, financial, social and environmental pressures are forcing many young farmers away from family farms all around the world, leaving the sector open to big-business interests and homogenization. The emerging Youth Food Movement, born at the Slow Food Congress in Mexico, November 2007, is bringing together the growing number of young people around the world who are actively seeking a better alternative mode of food production: from young farmers embracing local food traditions in my village of Molo in Kenya, to the rise of student-run convivia in the USA. 'Pangea: The Ark of Knowledge' is the movement's key project to proactively provide support and encouragement to young producers. It is a worldwide exchange program, in which students and young producers have the opportunity to learn through a placement with a skilled artisan producer/farmer, who exemplify the good, clean and fair approach. This is one further step in ensuring the passing on of traditional knowledge from small-scale farmers to the next generation. The Pangea exchange programs taking place across Europe and the United States will be reported on during the Terra Madre meeting this October, where a delegation of 1,000 young chefs, producers, farmers and students will meet for the very first time.

Kenyan Terra Madre food communities are already collaborating with Slow Food convivia and other allied organizations to promote sustainable agriculture and local food production as viable and rewarding vocations for young people. It is my hope that we will continue to strengthen these projects and collaboration to build a democratic farming system across Africa and the world, and to mitigate the impacts of the global food crisis on farming communities by building positive alternatives. As Carlo Petrini has said, 'An association which does not open its doors to youth is an association doomed to failure'.

Alice Waters

Vice-President Slow Food International

Jean-Anthelme Brillat-Savarin was right in 1825 when he wrote in his magnum opus, *La Physiologie du Goût*, that 'the destiny of nations depends on the manner in which they are fed'. Today in fact food production and distribution accounts for 60 percent of the world's economy and every decision we make about food has personal and global repercussions. It is generally conceded that the food we eat may be making us sick, but we have yet to acknowledge the environmental, political, cultural, social and ethical consequences of our national diet, not to mention side-effects such as soil depletion, water and air pollution, the loss of family farms and rural communities and even global warming.

When we pledge dietary allegiance to a fast food nation, there are also consequences for the health of our civil society and national character. When we eat fast food alone in our cars, we swallow the values of the corporations that manufacture them; namely that eating is no more important than fueling up and should be done quickly and anonymously.

As food will always be cheap and resources abundant, it's okay to waste. Feedlot beef, french fries and Coke are actually good for you. It doesn't matter where food comes from or how fresh it is because standardized consistency counts more than diversified quality. Since advertising confers value, in and of itself, it is seen as virtue, celebrity as virtual sainthood. Hard work—requiring concentration, application and honesty (cooking for the family, for example)—is seen as drudgery, of no commercial value.

No wonder our national attention span is so short: we get hammered with the message that everything in our lives should be fast, cheap and easy—especially food. So conditioned are we to believe that food should be almost free that even the rich grumble at the price of an organic peach: a fresh peach grown and picked by a local farmer who tends the land and pays his workers a fair wage. As my farmer friend David Mas Masumoto says, pound for pound peaches that good still cost less than Twinkies!

When we claim that eating well is an elitist concern, we cast a smokescreen over the fundamental role that our food decisions play in shaping the world. Eating well in this country costs more than eating poorly because we have a set of agricultural policies that subsidize fast food and make fresh wholesome food seem expensive. Organic foods seem elitist only because industrial food is kept artificially cheap. What America must learn are the 'slow food values' of the family meal, which teaches us, among other things, that the pleasures of the table are a social as well as a private good. Such values—moderation, conversation, tolerance, generosity and conviviality—are civic virtues. The pleasures of the table also beget responsibilities: to each other, to the animals we eat, to the land and to the people who work it. It follows that food that is healthy in every way will cost us more, in time and money, than we pay now. But when we have learned the real costs of food and the real rewards of eating, we will have laid a foundation not just for a healthier food system, but also for a healthier 21st-century democracy.

Vandana Shiva

Vice-President Slow Food International

The year 2008 has been significant for Slow Food, India and Navdanya.

I started Navdanya in 1987 to defend the freedom of seeds and the freedom of farmers to save and share them. These freedoms were threatened by GMOs and patents, including biopiracy patents such as those on Basmati rice. We won the case against the US company Ricetec, and Basmati is now a Slow Food Presidium.

Since 2003 Navdanya has been partnering Slow Food to build Slow Food India, and some of the members of our food communities are participating in Terra Madre in Turin. We have also started membership for schools, and there is of course Slow Food/Navdanya membership for co-producers (consumers).

For us, the seed-to-table/farm-to-kitchen integration is vital. If we have no seed diversity, we have no quality and no taste, no cultural diversity in food, no health and no nutrition. In March 2008, Navdanya organized a *Bija Yatra* (seed pilgrimage) from Champaran to Delhi, which covered 4000 km, met 400,000 farmers, and distributed 400 kg of different seeds. Champaran is the place where Gandhi started a *Satya-*

graha (Civil disobedience protest) against the forced cultivation of indigo. We see the forced cultivation of GMOs such as Bt-cotton as a slavery system, the way that of indigo used to be. It is pushing farmers to suicide. In India over the past decade, 200,000 farmers have committed suicide after becoming dependent on seeds from multinational corporations. This is why we have started a 'Seeds of Hope' campaign— to give small farmers freedom and hope.

Everyday in schools and communities, among farmers and policy-makers, we work for the cause of food freedom. Throughout the year we organize festivals and conferences devoted to biodiversity to make people aware of the richness we have received from nature and our heritage.

We also organize an annual gathering of seed keepers and organic producers called Vasundhera, an Indian equivalent of Terra Madre, and in December I am helping to organize Annam, a four-day National Festival for Food and Biodiversity, in Kerala.

The philosophy of Slow Food and Navdanya is a powerful antidote to the virus of junk food and the violence of industrial agriculture.

Paolo Di Croce

Secretary Slow Food International

Today a variety of definitions are used to describe us in every corner of the planet. For some, Slow Food is a political subject capable of bringing its influence to bear on environmental and agricultural matters. For others it is an apolitical subject, unaligned with the dominant ideologies because, like an NGO concerned with rural development projects in the South of the world, the issues and themes it addresses belong neither to the right nor to the left, but to everyone. For others still, it is a 'convivial movement' in which people share a passion for both eno-gastronomy and eco-gastronomy, or a publishing house or an event organizer or many other things besides. But we must never forget that Slow Food is first and foremost an association of thousands of people all round the world who, when they join, become members of a great international family and thus help spread its mission. At the base of it all are the local communities, the convivia, in which Slow Food takes root and through which it pursues its planetary aims. Slow Food today has about 100,000 members and more than a thousand convivia in 88 countries. The activities each convivium organizes to spread our philosophy are many and various. According to a rough estimate, each convivium stages an average of three to four events every year. This means a total of over 3,500 events a year, around ten a day, hence one every two hours or so. True, this is something of a simplistic vision of our organization, but I do believe it is one of many examples that convey an idea of what we are today, of our potential and, above all, of the outstanding work our convivia perform worldwide. The convivia are the promoters and ambassadors at a local level of the movement's needs and demands, but they also communicate their own members' requests. They involve the Terra Madre communities, organizing events of great ethical and social value. They use the products of Terra Madre communities in their area, thus supporting the local economy. They are the *trait d'union* between producers and conscious consumers (co-producers), without ever forgetting the 'defense of and the right to pleasure', which has always characterized the Slow Food association. They teach and educate co-producers so that they become more aware about the act of buying food, and they work in schools with children and teachers, in hospital canteens and in many other locations.

'Open the doors of the movement'—that was the message launched, loud and clear, by the Puebla Congress. 'Open them to everyone who believes in our association.' This task is entrusted primarily to the convivia and their leaders, because if the Slow Food family is to grow, it is necessary to involve everyone who shares our philosophy, who fights to defend biodiversity, who does not want to lose rural memory and wisdom, who believes young people have a fundamental role to play for the future of agriculture and the planet.

So many thanks to all of you, convivium leaders and members, who make it possible for us to grow, and to all those who will come in future and who will certainly find our 'doors open'.

Roberto Burdese

President Slow Food Italy

For many years, telling the story of Slow Food Italy meant telling the story of Slow Food as a whole.

Our association was founded in 1986 in the heart of Piedmont and, despite the fact that its international status was confirmed as far back as 1989 (with the signing of the Slow Food International Manifesto in Paris), for many years, the political and cultural reflections which lay behind it and charted its development, took place almost exclusively in Italy. The same applies to our most important projects. Until the end of the 1990s, Slow Food in Italy was almost exclusively a response to the critical situation that was becoming increasingly obvious in the farming and food sectors in Italy. The international dimension was seen by members and convivium leaders as an effective, mainly economic commitment to initiatives for the growth of Slow Food worldwide. It is evident, though, that Slow Food Italy has made a huge quantum leap thanks to the movement's international growth. Events like the Slow Food Award for the Defense of Biodiversity and its natural progression, Terra Madre, have been influencing the progress of Slow Food in Italy for some years now. Through such tangible opportunities to compare notes on an international scale, we Italian members have identified guidelines for our commitment and thus renewed our loyalty to the values which the Slow Food philosophy promotes.

Slow Food Italy now has more than 30,000 members, organized in almost 400 convivia (known in Italy as *condotte*) and 17 regional coordination bodies. The latter have been the most important organizational novelty in the Italian association. Indeed, it is thanks to collaboration among *condotte* in single regions that Slow Food Italy is able today to make its presence felt in every corner of the country. This is also why the association has managed, over the last four years, to esrablish 151 school gardens in as many Italian schools. The same applies to the Master of Food courses, which, in the last eight years, have involved about 40,000 people to become the most important food education project in the country! Italy's 179 presidia are also leading an increasingly active life thanks to the contribution and support of the regional coordination bodies and local *condotte*.

The new challenge is to find answers consistent with our philosophy to the question we are asked more and more frequently: how should we live and, more precisely, how should we eat, applying the principles of Slow Food in everyday life? The answer to the question resides in short food supply chain projects such as the Slow Food Earth Markets, but also in activities geared to improving the quality of food in canteens in hospitals, schools and workplaces. Many battles still have to be fought (the first of them is to reassert our 'No' to GMOs in farming and the food system). There is no lack of enthusiasm and being part of a truly democratic planetary network is certainly the added value that gives us the distinctive character of which we are increasingly proud.

Erika Lesser

Executive director Slow Food USA

From coast to coast, Americans are becoming more aware of the social, economic and environmental impact of our daily food choices. We live in a country of unimaginable but unsustainable bounty. Today farmers make up less than one percent of our population, and every minute we lose two acres of farmland to development. Obesity and diabetes are on the rise as the biodiversity of our food continues to shrink. Slow Food USA wants to change our food system. We envision a world in which everyone has access to delicious food that is good for them, good for the people who grow it and good for the planet. A growing number of Americans share that vision. In 2008, our member network has grown 20 percent and we now have more than 16,000 members in nearly 200 convivia in 47 states. Youth interest is growing. In colleges and universities, Slow Food on Campus convivia members take charge of their campus food systems by starting farmers' markets, sourcing local food for dining halls and fighting for fair treatment of farm workers. Together with young chefs, producers and activists, they also tap into Slow Food's Youth Network at events like Slow Food Nation and Terra Madre. Our Slow Food in Schools program also promotes many initiatives, including Garden-to-Table projects to teach children where food comes from and how it is produced. This year Slow Food USA awarded almost $10,000 in grants to enable Garden-to-Table leaders build websites and bread ovens and provide technical assistance to young chefs.

We are also addressing the issue of biodiversity. Over 1,000 food species and varieties are at risk of extinction in North America. To identify, restore and celebrate our diverse food traditions, in 2005 we formed the RAFT (Renewing America's Food Traditions) alliance of food, farming, environmental and culinary organizations. In May 2008, after three years of continentwide research, we published *Renewing America's Food Traditions: Saving and Savoring the Continent's Most Endangered Foods*, which tells the story of almost 100 foods, with recipes, research resources, an appendix of regional foods at risk and a toolkit for community-based conservation of heritage foods. Slow Food USA's work over the past eight years has continued to grow and today we are the second largest national association.

After focusing on increasing membership and creating awareness of the Slow philosophy in the US, in the past three years we have established national programs and partnerships with conservation, culinary and education institutions. Finally, in San Francisco from August 29 to September 1 2008, we staged Slow Food Nation, our antidote to the USA's reputation as a fast food nation. The event attracted farmers and producers from across the US and featured activities for all ages. Through such initiatives and our continuing work nationwide, we hope to introduce even more Americans to Slow Food.

☻ Otto Geisel

President Slow Food Germany

The Slow Food international movement lives on the one hand on its basic beliefs, widespread wherever the snail leaves its trail, and on the other on the vast cultural variety that comes to the fore when these beliefs are implemented in individual countries.

The theories of Carlo Petrini's 'neo-gastronomy' have been elaborated in Germany. Here we follow the networks principle with producers and consumers on a daily basis. It is worth fighting the battle for agro-biodiversity for our children's sake; the free availability of seeds is a political goal and our members are united by lean but continuous resistance to GMOs.

In spring 2008 the number of our members passed the 8,000 mark and we boast 70 convivia nationwide. Our second *Markt des guten Geschmacks*, a national food fair held in Stuttgart, attracted 65,000 visitors.

Today in Germany, Slow Food is recognized by everyone interested and familiar with responsible pleasure. Politicians and the media are forging contacts with us and our members are more motivated than ever.

We feel part of the global Slow Food family, but thanks to our country's cultural traditions, we also have our own distinctive character. At least on paper, every German school has had a school garden for the last 100 years. So our task is not to create school gardens, but to rescue them from neglect and to involve teachers and pupils actively.

Poor diet is a big problem for children in Germany. Slow Food and its convivia are working at a political and practical level on local projects such as pilot schemes for school cafeterias, hospitals and old people's homes.

Our national Ark of Taste has almost 30 'passengers'. This might not seem so many for such a large country, but each product has undergone a very careful selection process. The crops, animals and foods must either be at risk or have real chances of success on the market. For us, all this is not a matter of folklore, but of sustainable and responsible pleasure. Nowadays the message that Slow Food promotes the preservation of regional food sources is catching on. An increasing number of chefs are joining the organization, following the principle that everything in the kitchen must come from within a 50-kilometer radius. The media now understand that regionality is the best guarantee of quality.

Slow Food Germany is getting younger. We are recording a growing number of junior members and young families concerned about eating well. Slow Food groups have even sprung up spontaneously in various universities, for example in Dessau. We are very happy that there are so many German students at Pollenzo and Colorno, often the children of our members. Despite all the specificities of Slow Food Germany, we feel part in every sense part of a community with a global reach. When our members travel, they really do feel how the spirit that quickens Slow Food knows no national boundaries.

THE LAVAZZA COFFEE EXPERIENCE RETURNS TO THE SALONE DEL GUSTO

When someone fully shares your passions and your values, it's always best to stay close to them: this is why Lavazza will be waiting for you once again at this year's Salone del Gusto in Turin.

This edition brings lots of innovation:

- The Lavazza Coffee Design exhibition, featuring ten years of experimenting with coffee and all its forms, this is hosted in conjunction with the great Catalonian chef, Ferran Adrià, always a permanent guest at the Lavazza stand.

- The creative coffee workshops held by the Lavazza Training Centre, with guests including some of Italy's best-known chefs, such as Alfredo Russo, Giovanni Grasso and the famous maître chocolatier, Guido Gobino.

- Visitors can taste the new Lavazza espresso "A Modo Mio", in the various Lavazza coffee booths situated around the Salone.

SALONE DEL GUSTO 2008 Lingotto Fiere Torino - 23-27 October – Lavazza Stand – Pavillion 2

LAVAZZA MAIN SPONSOR
SALONE DEL GUSTO 2008

SALONE DEL GUSTO

ARMANDO TESTA

LAVAZZA
ITALY'S FAVOURITE COFFEE

www.lavazza.com

Rafael Pérez

President Slow Food Switzerland

Readers may well ask what is the point and what are the aims of Slow Food in a rich country like ours? Here in Switzerland, the standard of living is excellent, the per capita consumption of organic produce is the highest in the world, more than 100 presidium products are available in large-scale retail outlets and the majority of Swiss citizens supports *Gentechfrei*, the popular anti-GMO initiative.

So what is Slow Food doing in paradise?

The fact is that, in advanced societies like Switzerland, the de-culturization of food continues to spread, and only a small part of the enormous supply of food products can be described as 'good, clean and fair'. Behind the veneer of well-being of modern shopping malls lies an impoverishment of nature and of people. Even in wealthy Switzerland, every year many farming families are forced to abandon their land because, despite their hard work, they cannot earn enough to lead a decent life. Food is obviously losing its social function and cultural value. Fast and convenience ready-to-eat food continues to gain ground at the expense of biological variety and traditional artisan products.

In Switzerland, therefore, there is plenty of work to be done for the Slow Food movement, which has set itself the task of changing the food habits of a vast section of the population in a lasting way and converting it into a group of mature, responsible, sympathetic consumers. Assuming the responsibilities of the food we eat means overcoming a destructive consumer mentality.

True, this is no easy task, especially since we have nothing to sell but our ideas. Communication thus has an extremely important role to play—especially in a country with four official languages!

We are proceeding slowly but consistently. Slow Food is held in high esteem in Switzerland. Our opinion is sought by food producers, caterers and restaurateurs, in business associations and in universities. In the course of time, the ideas we have developed over the last 20 years have been understood by many. More and more frequently, we hear these concepts mentioned at conferences and seminars and see them quoted in the press. Slowing down is becoming a component of the quality of life. Adapting to natural rhythms is seen as a vital measure for combating the destruction of nature.

We are optimistic. Only a few years ago, less than 2 percent of the Swiss population had heard of Slow Food. More recent surveys suggest that the number has grown to 9 percent, the equivalent of 650,000 people.

The way ahead is clear. Let's enjoy the journey!

Silvija Davidson

Chair of the Slow Food UK Board of Directors

The UK has earned the epithet of 'Bad Food Britain', yet growing awareness of food provenance and eagerness to seek out and pay fairly for quality are much in evidence. As Geoff Andrews, author of *The Slow Food Story* avers, food is now at the top of most political agendas. The time is now ripe for Slow Food to make an impact in the UK. We already have over 2,000 members, and national association's task is to increase that number, harnessing, facilitating and amplifying the work of generally self-reliant convivia.

SFUK is a young organisation—its first Annual General Meeting took place in 2007— but directors and members alike have felt a sense of frustration that our path has not been a clear one and that progress has sometimes been painfully slow. We have tussled with issues of governance and staffing and the apparent ripeness for exploitation of the Slow Food 'brand', a testimony to the movement's growing reputation and the need to protect its good name and the clarity of its core message.

Our ambitious strategy now encompasses dedicated fundraising, recruitment to fill clearly identified roles, the creation of advisory boards and working parties, UK ownership of the *Snail Mail* newsletter (edited by Donald Reid with an advisory board that includes some of the UK's top food writers and campaigners) and exciting projects involving all our convivia. We also aim to increase the status of the UK Ark of Taste. Chair of Ark Suzanne Wynn has devised ways for convivia to achieve this and is creating an Ark Calendar to raise not only funds but also awareness of our endangered food heritage.

Our Events and Markets strategy will strengthen relationships between producers and co-producers and convey the concept of good, clean and fair food to a wide audience. Our involvement in four major BBC shows in 2008 has engendered a first-time bursary for producers who would not otherwise be able to exhibit. We have also developed closely defined criteria and parameters for exhibitors, which will also serve us well in other contexts. At London's Southbank Centre, for example, the Slow Food market interacts with the Southbank's charitable Learning and Participation project.

Two specific projects are: the Slow Bread campaign to raise awareness of the taste and health benefits of traditionally (slowly!) fermented breads and of the British baking and milling heritage; and the Heritage Orchards campaign to preserve traditional orchards and promote community orchards and school gardens. Both campaigns will involve all levels of the movement in UK and should prove income-generating and self-sustaining.

We are now confident of our way ahead. The Board comprises people with a wide range of skills and experience and has a good nationwide spread. If we manage to communicate clearly and inspiringly with members and exploit the opportunities that arise, we should see considerable growth in numbers, impact and influence.

Hirotoshi Wako

President Slow Food Japan

Last year several cases of fake food labeling were recorded in Japan. It was exactly this type of scandal that led to the creation of Slow Food Japan six years ago. However, rather than decreasing, such episodes are occurring in a growing number of sectors and have now become a serious national problem.

Moreover, in the current world crisis, calorie-wise, Japan is only 39 percent self-sufficient with regard to food production. In other words, we import 60 percent of our food. The main reason for this is the westernization of our eating habits. In the last 40 years, the annual per capita consumption of locally produced rice has halved, while consumption of meat, wheat and vegetable oils—mostly imported—has increased. Japan's post-war economic development led us to stop producing and start buying. What is more, we are buying badly: 30 percent of our food expenditure is spent on meals outside the home and 50 percent on ready-made meals.

The agricultural sector is experiencing a serious crisis: 2.6 percent of the population is 'feeding' the whole country. The average age of producers is rising and, for many of these producers, agriculture is a secondary source of livelihood. In this situation, Slow Food has developed rapidly, though, in 2007, the number of our members started to decrease. I thus decided to visit the various convivia to find out more about local realities and their problems. It wasn't easy to travel round the whole country, but I was rewarded by a warm welcome everywhere and I discovered some amazing local facts.

At Slow Food Iwate, for example, the market price of *tankaku* beef has increased thanks to its inclusion in the Ark of Taste, and producers have decided to donate a fixed sum to the convivium for each head of cattle sold. Elsewhere the young founders of the Slow Food Aichi Convivium played a successful role at the Nagoya Food Festival, so much so that they will be involved again in 2009. Examples like these made me understand that, though Slow Food Japan was initially only a trendy name, now a great number of people share our message.

Japan was the only country in Asia to be elected to the international board at the International Congress in Puebla. As well as involving greater responsibilities on the world stage, this role demands stability on a national level. It is a challenge that fills me with energy.

Last year, the Japanese government recognized Slow Food Japan as a non-profit organization. Since then, it has begun to collaborate with Zeri, a foundation which has been working on 'zero emissions' for years, to develop a number of food and environment projects. With it, in 2009, we intend to organize a major international Slow Food event. This is a great responsibility for us, but also a unique chance to start 'recovering the earth'.

Jean Lhéritier

President Slow Food France

We are now a global network that looks at gastronomy and food with new eyes. Slow Food has succeeded in putting together visions of food culture which are each very different, in stimulating concerns and energies to achieve change. Each one of us can identify with the idea that it is possible to improve the food we eat by implementing a new model of farming, respecting cultures and heritages and refusing to accept a rigid definition of gastronomy.

France is often perceived as the homeland of old-fashioned traditional gastronomy, as a country that struggles to keep up with a changing world. All the actions and strategies of the French association express the desire to take change on board in a non-elitist way, to benefit as many people as possible. The priority today is to eat *Slow-ly*.

Which is why, in April 2008, during the municipal elections, we appealed to the elected representatives to promote greater food quality in collective catering according to five precise commitments. The signatories include Bertrand Delannoë, mayor of Paris.

This year we also organized the second National Slow Food Day, in which a specific theme combines with our desire to encourage the general public to find out about

our initiatives and our philosophy. Whereas, in 2007, the theme was potatoes, on September 27 we staged tastings of and debates about raw milk cheese. As in the past, in the course of National Slow Food Day, the theme chosen was promoted by 30-40 convivia in the various towns and regions of France.

Finally, for the third year running, on September 7-8, in Clermont-Ferrand (Auvergne), we held our Summer University (organized in the Basque Country in 2006 and in Dijon in 2007): two days of reflection and in-depth analysis, open to members and non-members alike, about how raw milk adds flavor to cheese and the type of farming required to achieve this.

High food quality in collective catering, the second Slow Food Day and the third Slow Food Summer University—this is Slow Food France's program to make each one of us realize that eating better means eating simply and, if we devote time to food, culture and solidarity. In short, it means eating *Slow-ly*. In 2009 we shall repeat the initiatives and expand them. From November 27-30 2009, we shall also celebrate a new event in the annual Slow Food calendar: Eurogusto, the European gastronomy biennial, which will be held in Tour, in the Loire Valley.

Leonie Furber

Slow Food International Councilor, Australia

Australia is bringing the Slow Food philosophy to life in communities spread across its vast territory, home to diverse populations and environments. The convivia and their projects — from camp stove cook-offs to city film festivals, from bush-tucker workshops to pizza making in school gardens — are starting to fully represent the nation.

As a young country, we take strength from the opportunity to be innovative, whilst honouring the traditions of indigenous and settler cultures. Our multi-cultural community brings together the original Aboriginal nations, descendants of the British colonisers and numerous migrant groups from all round the world. Today, we are a melting pot of race and creed and this can be seen in all aspects of life, not least in our food culture.

Thirty-six convivia are active across every state and territory of Australia and our current membership of more than 2,000 is the fastest growing in the world. However, without a national association we have not had a strong national voice or support network for the convivia. To this end, we have been working towards the formation of an association—which was approved in June 2008—and have developed a proposal for significant national projects which strive to capture the imagination of members and the broader community. Among these, the 'Slow Knowledge' communications project— with publications from *A Slow Food Guide to Australia* to *Slow Food at the Edge of the World*, recording the diversity of food brought to Australia by immigrants—will collect information from the Slow world; the learning-by-practice 'Dirty Hands' project will improve food, health and ecological knowledge through the development of school and community gardens, and Heliculture 1 will promote membership in universities and among young Australians.

We wish to see more endangered food products added to the Australian Ark of Taste and the development of the first presidium projects in our country, and we intend to collaborate with indigenous communities through the 'Bush Know-How' project to help sustain native food diversity and increase consumer awareness and market opportunities. Finally, we are very excited to launch '23° Slow' to link Slow Food communities bisected by the Tropic of Capricorn—from Brazil, to Fiji to Australia—fostering the exchange of ideas and information and raising awareness and action around indigenous foods, biodiversity and culture. To further develop Slow Food in our country, we are planning the first Australian version of Terra Madre, Terra Australis, to be followed in the future by the regional Terra Oceania.

Are these projects vastly different from current convivium activities? The answer is yes and no. Convivia around Australia are building their membership and engaging with communities through events and programs, but at a very local level without broader coordination or collaboration. The new projects will open the Australian membership and community to new possibilities and horizons, and we hope Slow Food Australia will help Slow Food to grow intelligently and make a real difference worldwide.

Jan Wolf

President Slow Food Netherlands

In its early years Slow Food in The Netherlands focused on the enjoyment of good food and wine; considerations about biodiversity came later.

Slow Food has now matured into a movement in which the quality of food is the central issue, and producers and con-sumers have an equally important role in maintaining and developing that quality. The future of food is our concern, and we therefore strongly support the development of the Youth Food Movement in The Netherlands.

Most of our members love good food and are eager to know more about its production. Likewise, Slow Food members who are producers love to meet the people who enjoy the results of their work and teach them how to distinguish between mediocre food and really good quality.

The activities of Slow Food Netherlands are thus tailored to these demands: on top of regular convivium activities and the development of youth activities, we also focus on printed and digital information, educational projects and events. With the help of all our members we intend to publish a yearly guide of producers, restaurants and shops where the food is good, clean and fair. Other spearheads are the development of a quarterly magazine and the improvement of our website. A successful pilot project was launched in 2007 called Slow

Wave. In it younger children learned about food and taste and practiced cooking techniques. The project ended with a competition between the participating schools. In 2009 it will be made available to all convivia. For adults we will develop a Dutch version of Slow Food Italy's Master of Food program: courses on specific subjects, focused on knowledge and accompanied by tasting sessions and, where necessary, practical cooking lessons. Some 4,000 visitors came to Terra Madre Nederland, held for the first time on May 17-18 2008. Featuring a producers' market, workshops, a restaurant, enoteca, workshops and seminars, the event proved a huge success. A second edition will be held in autumn 2009.

Food production in The Netherlands is very much under the influence of the industrial paradigm, the popularity of convenience foods and the demands of hygiene regulations. Helping small-scale producers to continue working on the products they love to make will be a focal point of our work in the coming years.

Cristina Gaitan Buckard

Chair of Slow Food Swedish Ark Comission

We were baking seven different kinds of cookie for a 'coffee party', and we persuaded Lotta, a real baker, to make *Upplandskubb*, a product on the Swedish Ark of Taste, a bread that is steamed not baked. Lotta only had two moulds, but she eventually managed to produce 124 loaves.

This all happened in August 2007, when the weather was warm and sunny. Food artisans from across the country were in Stockholm to display and sell their products, and Slow Food Sweden had a stand of its own to present its initiatives. We now have nearly 600 members and 14 convivia.

Upplandskubb originates from the Stockholm/Uppsala region, where it brings back childhood memories for young and old alike. As it hadn't been on sale since the 1960s, that day last year the stories of when and where people used to eat it and who used to bake it seemed as though they'd never stop. We thus spread culinary pleasure and memory. As the supply was limited, we tried raising the price to slow down sales. It didn't work: the *Upplandskubb* sold like hotcakes! All of a sudden it was easy for us to explain what 'good, clean

and fair' really means. The mission of the Ark of Taste was clear to all. From now on Slow Food in Sweden will be remembered as the savior of *Upplandskubb* and a top quality baker. Five convivia collaborated to convey the Slow Food philosophy over the three days of the event.

But how are we going to improve access to good, clean and fair food in a country as focused on industrialized food production as Sweden is? I am not without hope. The Swedish Government has ruled that organic food consumption must account for 25 percent of total food consumption by 2010. More and more consumers are demanding organic products. Direct purchases from farmers, community-supported agriculture and organic box schemes are increasing. Farmers' markets and food festivals offering locally produced products are gaining popularity. Artisan products are enjoying better exposure in commercial retail outlets. Media coverage is intensifying on the quality of school meals and food for the elderly.

The theme of good, clean and fair food was also discussed in various workshops by members, artisans, farmers, fishermen, scientists and chefs at Terra Madre Sweden, held in Falkoping in 2007. Local delicacies were served for lunch and aquavit was offered as an evening aperitif. By tradition, Swedes have to sing when they make a toast with aquavit. After you drink and sing you get thirsty, so you drink and sing all over again and again and again ...

At Falkoping we formalized a vision: 'Everyone must have the right to good, clean and fair food'. We agreed that to make this vision materialize, we need to learn more, theoretically and practically, about our food and our food culture. Producers also have to realize that they can count on our support as 'co-producers' of food quality. The time has come!

◉ Raúl Hernández Garciadiego

Councilor for Latin America, Mexico

Last year Puebla hosted the 5th International Slow Food Congress, an event rich in symbolism. During his opening speech, Carlo Petrini proposed that the congress express its solidarity with the state of Tabasco, totally submerged by a disastrous flood, and provide help for the cacao producers of the area. His words and the applause they generated triggered profound ethical reflection.

In his summing-up speech, the President of Slow Food International talked about the setting up of the Tehuacán Mixteca Popoloca Convivium whose 1,100 members, all farmers and indigenous people, immediately made it the association's most numerous convivium. When the congress was over, many delegates visited the Tehuacán Valley Convivium in an area that produces corn, beans, amaranth, *chile*, squash and more besides,

and found out about the various irrigation and rainwater collection techniques. The latter are part of the tradition and heritage of the countries of Central America and today are regenerating nature through the so-called 'Water Forever' project.

The members of the convivium are families who grow amaranth in the states of Puebla and Oaxaca. At the Puebla congress they presented their foods, made using traditional tools such as the hand-mill for grinding corn, the *comales* used to make *tortillas* and the clay pots used to make sauces and stews. We were amazed at the colors and flavors of the foods served to us with such kindness and pride, while dancers and musicians made the occasion even more enjoyable. The essence of 12,000 years of history captured with same spirit of conviviality that brought Slow Food into life in the first place.

◉ Roberta Marins de Sá

International Councilor for Brazil

We organized the first Terra Madre Brazil in October 2007 with the support of the Ministry of Agrarian Development.

Having been a volunteer at Terra Madre 2004, and knowing how much work was involved, it seemed a natural step to help find volunteers for the event in Brazil. In the end, 35 students were chosen from various areas. In most cases, they were

coming into contact with the principles of Slow Food for the first time. In this way, the movement in Brazil received a very special gift: the strength and enthusiasm of young people. Since these youngsters joined Slow Food, some interesting things have been accomplished, especially the Brasilia Convivium's participation in the Brasil Sabor 2008 food festival.

There it was these new members who displayed a potential that must and can be developed. For the opening of the festival, they used produce from local communities, the Ark of Taste and the Presidia, to produce delicious new dishes. We talked to the public about 'ecogastronomy', sustainable food and the possibility of producing food using alternative methods. In the workshops, designed for adults and children alike, the contribution of our young members was fundamental, as it was they who presented and organized the sessions. Not that it's easy to work with 30 kids aged between four and eight, and keep them occupied for two hours in a shop-ping mall packed with distractions! The great thing was that, at the end of the day, the children didn't want to go home. Today the challenge is to keep alive the interest and the enthusiasm of this group of young people, which is so important for the future of the Slow Food movement in Brazil and in the world. The path to follow will be to give more autonomy to convivium activities and encourage youngsters to become convivium leaders and bring them closer to the food communities. The Youth Food Movement and the inclusion of young people in the Terra Madre network will undoubtedly constitute a new phase of growth for the movement.

Danilau Ihar

Belarus Convivium Leader

The first Belarusian Slow Food convivium was created in 2004. That was when Carlo Petrini's profound words about the importance of native breed and species protection—the basis of the biodiversity and food safety of any country—reached us from Italy.

We became interested in the idea of reviving and preserving our national customs and traditions of food production, of connecting consumers and producers to provide the former with good, clean and fair food.

These are problems that have been worrying Belarusian scientists, ecologists, journalists, farmers and simple citizens for some time now.

The creation of the first Belarusian Slow Food convivium was the result of close cooperation among many people, and its members took an active part in the Terra Madre world meeting of food communities in 2004 and 2006. During the event, we had the chance to meet a lot of farmers and share our experience with traditional food producers, scientists and cooks from all over the world. The creative atmosphere of Terra Madre inspired the Belarusian delegation to undertake various activities back home.

Since 2004 we have increased the number of convivium members to 81; organized a press conference with regional coordinator Lilia Smelkova in Minsk, the capital of Belarus, widely covered by local newspapers; initiated a food expedition round Belarus to identify and protect local produce and dishes; organized five visits of convivium members, journalists and guests to Belarusian villages to taste regional cuisine; set up the the Wild Fruit and Infusions of Rosson Presidium, the first in Belarus, which was present at the Salone del Gusto 2006; edited, published and mailed Snail - the symbol of good taste, the first Slow Food newsletter for CIS countries, to Russian-speaking convivia; organized the first meeting of Belarusian farmers, cooks and scientists to enable them to swap views and ideas. We plan to develop the Wild Fruit and Infusions of Rosson Presidium and to take its produce to the Salone del Gusto 2008; to continue the nationwide food expedition and recount its results to the mass media; to publish the second and third numbers of our newsletter.

We are open to cooperate with all of you and invite other convivia and anyone else interested in the first Belarusian convivium to take part in its activities. We are also keen to develop farm holidays in Belarus. We hereby invite readers take part in gastronomic tours round our country, where you will meet a lot of people who think the same way as you do, admire the natural beauty and discover local natural produce. All this will help spread the philosophy of Slow Food Belarus outside the country.

We will be grateful for any support—in word and deed! We are full of enthusiasm to revive and support Belarusian agriculture and farming, to help it to produce good, clean and fair food and sell it to consumers at reasonable prices. Let us all get together to revive the Mother Earth of Belarus!

MOTHER EARTH

SNAILS ARE FRIENDS OF VINEYARDS, WHICH LED US TO IDENTIFY BUNCHES OF GRAPES AS FURTHER FOOD FOR THOUGHT.

ENO-ECO-NEO
A STORY
IN THREE ACTS

John Irving
UK, writer and contributor to Slow Food publications
Photos Alberto Peroli

ENO

The Snail moves slowly, teaching us that speed makes men rash and foolish.
Francesco Angelita, *I pomi d'oro* (1607)

My cuttings file contains an article, frayed and turning yellow at the edges, that I took from the British daily *The Guardian* in 1989. It's at once a historical piece and a piece of history. It describes a strange new movement founded by a group of friends in a small town in the North of Italy: an 'eno-gastronomic' (food and wine to you and me) movement whose aim was to defend quality food, the right to pleasure, conviviality and slow living. Defining the experience, the group leader Carlo Petrini spoke of 'insane folly'. Not surprisingly, the London journalist who wrote the article seemed a little taken aback.

According to my reckoning, this must have been one of the first articles to talk to the English-speaking world about Slow Food. After all, the Slow Food International Movement came into being the same year the piece appeared at the Opera Comique in Paris, where delegates from 20 countries got together to sign a Manifesto written by the poet and intellectual Folco Portinari.

'We are enslaved by speed and have all succumbed to the same insidious virus: *Fast Life*,' recites the sacred text. *Slowfoodistas* had nothing to lose but their chains. 'May suitable doses of guaranteed sensual pleasure and slow, long-lasting enjoyment preserve us from the contagion of the multitude who mistake frenzy for efficiency'.

Slow Food saw food in a broad sense—ingredients, products, consumption— as the apotheosis of whole cultures and personal pleasures. To support the philosophy, in 1996 the international Salone del Gusto exhibition and *Slow – Herald of Taste and Culture* made their debuts. The journal in particular was slow in name and in fact. The first number was a paean to everything snail-paced: from the gastropod itself to the Argentine tango and the Spanish ritual of the *tapa*. 'When

Mediterranean Conferences are organized and a suitable umbrella theme is required,' wrote Manuel Vázquez Montalbán, one of the early supporters of the movement, 'I cannot understand why nobody ever thought about proclaiming *tapa* the food expression of a lifestyle that involves giving things a try, chatting all the while, drinking with discernment and reaching the unusual conclusion that, in small portions, the world is beautiful.'

Slowness as a lifestyle then. Montalbán was a distinguished name and his adhesion was an effective advertisement for the movement. The first number of *Slow* was rounded off by *In Praise of Slowness*, in which Carlo Petrini expatiated on the movement's elected symbol, the snail, before surveying new vistas, apparently far away but actually nearer than they seemed. 'Snails are friends of vineyards, which led us to identify bunches of grapes as further food for thought ... our planet is gradually being strapped in by increasingly long and dense rows of vines. No space is off-limits.' It was the mid 90s and 'eno' was already turning into 'eco'.

ECO

Agriculture, agriculture ... and more agriculture. *That* is what we are talking about.
Cinzia Scaffidi, *Slow* 45.

It was inevitable that Slow Food should broaden its outlook to embrace, besides the quality of life, the very survival of planet earth. In *Slow* 17, the editor Alberto Capatti wrote that, 'Slow Food is an association that shuns costume pageants and the rituals that are recorded in the annals of gastronomy. It does not encourage the cult of "historic" foods and menus, yet it is profoundly linked to the values of the land and the past. The preservation of typical products, the protection of species from genetic manipulation, the cultivation of memory and taste education—

these are all aspects of this passion of ours for time [...] A fistful of buckwheat in a soup, a smidgeon of nutmeg, the smoke arising from grilled meat— these are all traces that lead us back to the past; traces of humanity. Let's follow them'.

To cut a long story short, it was precisely by following those traces that Slow Food understood that conviviality is beautiful—not to say indispensable—but also that, once the meal's over, it's a healthy habit to take a constitutional in the country. If need be, getting its hands dirty and sticking its neck out. Its slogan became 'Defend Agrobiodiversity' and it pledged to protect traditional foods and primary ingredients, conserving processing and cultivation methods and defending domestic and wild species, breeds and varieties. The association combined respect, study and knowledge of eno-gastronomic culture to support all those seeking to produce food sustainably, wherever they happened to be in the world. As it internationalized, so Slow Food had to address new problems, explore new territories and savour new cuisines. Taking things a step at a time is fine but no one could argue that the step from *tajarin* to basmati rice wasn't a big one. To make the path easier, Slow Food invented, in chronological order: the Ark of Taste, which identifies, catalogues and describes almost forgotten flavours; the Presidia, which support small-scale quality food products, endangered native animal breeds and ancient fruit and vegetable varieties, raise the profile of local areas, recover traditional crafts and manufacturing techniques; the Slow Food Award for the Defence of Biodiversity, set up in 2000 to recognise and support research, production, marketing and cataloguing activities in favour of agro-biodiversity. 2004 saw the birth of a close relative of the Slow Award: the innovative, almost revolutionary Terra Madre event. To this 'international meeting of food communities' Slow Food invited 'intellectuals of land and sea' with all their baggage of

INFORMED AND UPDATED ABOUT WHERE, HOW, WHY AND BY WHOM FOOD IS PRODUCED, NEO-GASTRONOMES DON'T SEE THEMSELVES AS CONSUMERS BUT AS 'CO-PRODUCERS'.

wisdom and knowledge, representatives of the millions of people who produce food but also respect quality, the planet and human labour. After getting to know each other, participants kept in touch and gave rise to a vast network. Terra Madre, Mother Earth and the mother of all networks, a model of dialogue, brotherhood and solidarity.

HRH the Prince of Wales summed it all up in his closing speech at the first Terra Madre event. 'The food you produce is far more than just food, for it represents an entire culture—the culture of the family farm. It represents the ancient tapestry of rural life; the dedicated animal husbandry, the struggle with the natural elements, the love of landscape, the childhood memories, the knowledge and wisdom learnt from parents and grandparents, the intimate understanding of local climate and conditions, the hopes and fears of succeeding generations. Ladies and gentlemen, all of you represent genuinely sustainable agriculture and I salute you.'

NEO

Eating is an agricultural act
Wendell Berry

The elaboration of the theory of a cultivated, eco-sensitive neo-gastronomy—invoking freedom of choice, education, a multidisciplinary approach to food and eating—wasn't a step forward from eco-gastronomy. It was a parallel and logical offshoot. Its manifesto is Carlo Petrini's book *Slow Food Nation*. Its banner is the University of Gastronomic Sciences in Pollenzo/Colorno.

Informed and updated about where, how, why and by whom food is produced, neo-gastronomes don't see themselves as consumers but as 'co-producers', active subjects who identify with all the implications and consequences of their buying choices. For them, food must be good clean and

fair. Good, hence tasty, fresh, seasonal, capable of pleasing the senses. Clean, hence produced without damaging the earth's resources, without harming human health. Fair, hence respectful of social justice, meaning fair pay and decent workplace conditions for everyone involved in the short supply chain: from production to commercialisation to consumption.

Neo-gastronomes adopt a critical but constructive approach to eating. They are passionate about food and wine but also want to save the world's agro-biodiversity. For the neo-gastronome, eating isn't only a biological necessity but also a convivial pleasure to be shared with others and a form of responsible consumption that exerts a direct effect on the market, hence on food production. And teaching the senses, all five of them, to understand and appreciate food and all it represents is a way of sharpening our awareness of the world around us.

Keyword
CONVIVIUM

This Latin noun (plural: convivia)evokes the verb *cum vivere*, 'to live together'. Slow Food chose the word 'convivium' to denote the local groups into which its members are organized. The convivia organize tastings and seminars, promote the association's campaigns at a local level, defend local foods, activate taste education projects in schools and participate in major Slow Food international events.

Keyword
FOOD COMMUNITY

The term was coined for the first Terra Madre event and refers to the extended food supply chain. From seed and breed graders through to retailers—all the artisans quality food needs to be produced, distributed and consumed, hence to be an economic, environmental, social and cultural resource.

QUATER

IL PRIMO VINO
QUATTRO VOLTE AUTOCTONO
ESTREMA ESSENZA DI SICILIA

L'unione delle quattro varietà autoctone racchiude "in un solo vino" l'essenza dell'intera terra di Sicilia e della sua ineguagliabile biodiversità.

FIRRIATO

SLOW FOOD, A MOVEMENT CAPABLE OF DEVELOPING NEW PROJECTS AND NEW IDEAS AND ADDRESSING NEW CHALLENGES, OWES ITS DYNAMISM TO THE ENERGY OF ITS MEMBERS

BALANCING ACT

Michael Dimock
USA, President of the Roots of Change Fund, which collaborates with Slow Food in California. He is past President of Slow Food USA and founder of the Russian River Convivium

NETWORK

The Slow Food movement is a global network. Its impact on media, culture and communities seeking a good, clean and fair food system testifies to the power of the network. To continue building on success, it is important to understand the nature of the network, what it is and how to optimize its effects.

Simply put, a network is a system of intersection points (nodes) and flow routes (links). Applied to human dynamics, a 'social' network describes the relationship between the nodes (individuals and their organizations) and the links (common purpose, values, principles, information and activities). The network is free of impeding bureaucratic structures and this freedom increases effectiveness and accelerates progress. The network's vitality is important in a time when rapid innovation is required to supplant currently destructive components of the food system devised in an earlier time and that now threaten the future of our small planet. Networks have become important because

people have come to understand the concept of the 'network effect', which says that the value of a network grows in proportion to the number of nodes and links. One person talking to five others in one year and implementing one small project has some effect. In contrast, 80,000 people each talking to 20 others in a year and together implementing 1,000 larger projects has, relatively speaking, a quantum effect.

It may seem ironic that individualism, which also has negative qualities, is a key positive dynamic that has permitted the emergence of powerful networks. Unprecedented levels of education, wide access to information technology, the quantity and quality of information itself and the diminishing influence of traditional social conventions support the individual's ability to join a network. Every person can form their own opinion, start their own project and rally others to join them using email, websites and cell phones. People also feel free to leave one network and join another at any time.

THROUGH A NETWORK ONE CAN COMMUNICATE VALUES AND BELIEFS THAT WILL AGGREGATE A COMMUNITY OF COMMON INTEREST, PEOPLE MOTIVATED BY VISIONS OR BELIEFS.

NEW PROJECTS

NEW VALUES

The network is powerful but its fluidity of participation requires certain forms of nurturing to keep it intact and operative. The self-directed nature of modern people means that effective leadership does not emerge from coercion and control. Good network leaders are more like stewards, coaches or mentors who discover motivation, channel energy and facilitate meaningful collaborative action. Through a network one can communicate values and beliefs that will aggregate a community of common interest, people motivated by visions or beliefs. Communication comes in different forms: person-to-person contact and mass media; visual and auditory; written and spoken; paper and electronic. All these forms are needed to communicate to people and organizations. Some of those receiving a communication for the first time at the edge of a network and who share the beliefs will become attracted. They will become attuned to the information flowing in the network. Many who are tuned in and enlivened by the communication will support the network's activity or purpose and some will seek to lead a node of activity in a specific space or place. The edge of the network grows.

With each added node more information flows, more opportunities to act and more potential points of contact with the world emerge. Each person and organization in the network creates a sub-network. Thus, the interface with the world expands exponentially with the addition of each new node.

Slow Food's development reflects this dynamic. In its earliest days, when the Ark of Taste and presidia were launched, the Slow Food movement, mostly in Europe and North America, provided people passionate about food a way to become meaningfully involved in activities that enlarged the supply of 'good' food in their own communities. The purpose of preserving and the act of promoting defined the network and bound the nodes. Those sharing an interest came into the network as they learned about it through events and publications.

Slow Food has grown the network by broadening its purpose to include more values, principles and projects. Eco-gastronomy and Terra Madre birthed new nodes and links, reaching all around the world. These additions to the intellectual and practical core of the movement pushed Slow Food's focus beyond just 'good' food. It now also includes 'clean' and 'fair' food. This expansion of purpose allowed social justice and environmental advocates to align with Slow Food and to initiate new forms of meaningful action. Terra Madre linked communities north and the south. In the same way, eco-gastronomy has formed links to universities, social justice and environmental NGOs. The network has become more powerful.

ORDER AND CHAOS

Still the question remains, how does Slow Food maximize the network effect and accelerate transformation of the food system?

ECO-GASTRONOMY AND TERRA MADRE HAVE GIVEN BIRTH TO NEW NODES AND LINKS ALL AROUND THE WORLD.

DEVELOPING
NEW IDEAS

The answer lies in an additional concept related to network dynamics. Successful networks mimic nature by permitting a harmonious balance of chaos and order to optimize creative innovation or evolution. The Slow Food movement must find the balance between chaos and order or anarchy and control, as ceptions, biases and preferences. One person cannot effectively decide what is best for the whole food system. Many eyes, hearts and minds are needed to deal with the complex reality now faced. Thus, as a network steward, I fight my first impulse and work to let go of control. Instead, I work with my colleagues to create a convivial at-

ADDRESSING
NEW CHALLENGES

Carlo Petrini would say it. This means, Slow Food must distribute leadership and allow the nodes to govern and implement action themselves without impeding their progress.

This central challenge may be more art than science. It requires trust, faith and patience. It requires that stewards of the network and leaders of the nodes allow themselves to endure the tension of the opposites and to find the razor's edge of balance. It requires that those involved allow their hearts and minds to work in harmony.

I know, for me, the first impulse is to control activities based on my own belief about how to achieve the desired outcomes. Yet I am but one person living within a complex system. I will make many mistakes based on my personal partial perception, misper-

mosphere with good communication, trust and clarity on goals. When we do this well, those in our network find a healthy balance between chaos and order and maximize creativity in their innovative actions on the ground in their locales.

In the years ahead, Slow Food must nurture the network's links with clear communication, good information and meaningful opportunities to collaborate, but also empower the network by allowing the nodes to make manifest the common purpose, values and principles of Slow Food in diverse ways all around the world. By doing this well, Slow Food will become an even more vital force, accelerating change in a many-faceted global movement seeking a good, clean and fair food system.

SUSTAINABLE COMMUNITIES

Fritjof Capra
Austria, physicist, systems theorist and writer

NETWORK

In recent years, networks have become a major focus of attention in science, in business and also in society at large and throughout a newly emerging global culture. In science, the focus on networks began in the 1920s, when ecologists viewed ecosystems as communities of organisms, linked together in network fashion through feeding relations, and used the concept of food webs to describe these ecological communities. As the network concept became more and more prominent in ecology, systemic thinkers began to use network models at all systems levels, viewing organisms as networks of cells and cells as networks of molecules, just as ecosystems are understood as networks of individual organisms. Correspondingly, the flows of matter and energy through ecosystems were perceived as the continuation of the metabolic pathways through organisms.

In this essay, I discuss the fundamental role of networks in the organization of all living systems, and I highlight the similarities and differences between biological and social networks.

SELF-GENERATING

The defining characteristic of a living system is its metabolism, the ceaseless flow of energy and matter through a network of chemical reactions, which enables the system to continually generate, repair and perpetuate itself. The understanding of metabolism has two basic aspects. One is the continuous flow of energy and matter, the other is the network of chemical reactions. One of the most important insights of the new understanding of life that is now emerging at the forefront of science is the recognition that the network is a pattern that is common to all life. Wherever we see life, we see networks.

Closer examination of these living networks has shown that their key characteristic is that they are self-generating. In a cell, for example, biological structures are continually produced, repaired and regenerated by the cellular network. Similarly, at the level of a multicellular organism, the bodily cells are continually regenerated and recycled by the organism's metabolic network. Living networks continually create or recreate themselves by transforming or replacing their components. In this way they undergo

continual structural changes while preserving their web-like patterns of organization.

IDEAS LIKE MOLECULES

Life in the social realm can also be understood in terms of networks. Social networks, however, are not networks of chemical reactions; they are networks of communications. Like biological networks, they are self-generating, but what they generate is mostly non-material. Each communication creates thoughts and meaning, which give rise to further communications and thus the entire network generates itself. The dimension of meaning is crucial to understand social networks. Even when they generate material structures—such as material goods, artifacts or works of art—these material structures are very different from the ones produced by biological networks. They are usually produced for a purpose, according to some design, and they embody some meaning. Let us now juxtapose biological and social networks. Biological systems exchange molecules in networks of chemical reactions; social systems exchange information and ideas in networks of communications. Thus, biological networks operate in the realm of matter, whereas social networks operate in the realm of meaning.

SOCIAL NETWORKS

Both types of networks produce material structures. The metabolic network of a cell produces the cell's structural components, and it also generates molecules that are ex-

BIOLOGICAL SYSTEMS EXCHANGE MOLECULES IN NETWORKS OF CHEMICAL REACTIONS; SOCIAL SYSTEMS EXCHANGE INFORMATION AND IDEAS IN NETWORKS OF COMMUNICATIONS.

changed between the network's nodes as carriers of energy or information or as catalysts of metabolic processes. Social networks, too, generate their structural components—buildings, roads, technologies and so on—and they also produce material goods and artifacts that are exchanged between the network's nodes. In addition, social systems produce non-material structures. Their processes of communication generate shared rules of behavior, as well as a shared body of knowledge. The rules of behavior, whether formal or informal, are known as social structures and are the main focus of social science. The ideas, values, beliefs and other forms of knowledge generated by social systems constitute structures of meaning, which may be called semantic structures.

In modern societies, the culture's semantic structures are documented—that is, materially embodied—in written and digital texts. They are also embodied in artifacts, works of art and other material structures, as they are in traditional non-literate cultures. Indeed, the activities of individuals in social networks specifically include the organized production of material goods. All these material structures—texts, works of art, technologies and material goods—are created for a purpose and according to some design. They are embodiments of the shared meaning generated by the society's networks of communications.

Finally, biological and social systems both generate their own boundaries. A cell produces and sustains a membrane, which imposes constraints on the chemistry that takes place inside it. A social network, or community, produces and sustains a non-material cultural boundary, which imposes constraints on the behavior of its members.

The extension of the systemic conception of life to the social domain, which I have briefly outlined in this essay, explicitly includes the material world. For social scientists, this may be unusual because. traditionally, the social sciences have not been very interested in the world of matter. Our academic disciplines have been organized in such a way that the natural sciences deal with material structures, while the social sciences deal with social structures, which are understood to be, essentially, rules of behavior.

In the future, this strict division will no longer be possible because the key challenge of our time—for social scientists, natural scientists and everyone else—will be to build ecologically sustainable communities. A sustainable community is designed in such a way that its technologies and social institutions—its material and social structures—do not interfere with nature's inherent ability to sustain life. In other words, the design principles of our future social institutions must be consistent with the principles of organization that nature has evolved to sustain the web of life. A unified conceptual framework for the understanding of material and social structures, such as the one outlined in this essay, will be essential for this task.

WHERE THERE IS LIFE, THERE ARE NETWORKS.

BROTHERHOOD

Samuel Karanja Muhunyu
Kenya, Slow Food Central Rift Convivium leader

NETWORK

It all started with a visit to Kenya by two Slow Food officials, Cinzia Scaffidi and Ugo Vallauri, in June 2004. On the 21st of the same month, they visited Molo in Central Rift where the organization Network for Eco-farming in Africa (NECOFA) had organized a food fair on indigenous foods in their honor. Molo is situated in the Mau highlands in the Central Rift Valley about 210 km northwest of Nairobi. It is at a high altitude (over 2,500 meters above sea level) with high rainfall (2,500–3,000 mm per annum) and rich, deep, clay loam soil. The area is agriculturally rich with a temperate climate. These factors attracted European settlers during the colonial period and many of them established large-scale farming in the area, hence the Central and North Rift Valley's nickname, the 'White Highlands'. Today the area is regarded as the country's 'grain basket', producing over 50 percent of its staple foods, such as maize, potatoes, wheat and so on.

CULTURE CANCELLATION

Molo and the Central Rift Valley are largely multiethnic, since large-scale European farmers, the forest department and the railway cooperation used to draw labor from different communities all over the country. After independence in 1963, many of these large-scale farmers abandoned Kenya, leaving the way open for small-scale farmers, mainly former laborers (and their descendants) who, as members either of cooperatives or of government settlement schemes, acquired and subdivided the large farms. The different communities brought with them rich and diverse food cultures, not that this, unfortunately, was of any benefit to them. On the contrary, forces such as modernity, colonialism, educa-

ARCHIVIO SLOW FOOD

TERRA MADRE
NETWORK

tion and even religion conspired to convince them that their food cultures, based mainly on indigenous foods, were inferior and backward. Gradually but steadily, these food cultures were 'eroded' in favor of foreign, especially western, food cultures. The more 'educated' and those in close contact with the settler families led this 'erosion' process, which continued until most of the country was 'infected' and the majority of Kenyans lost pride and confidence in their indigenous food cultures.

SOLIDARITY

The Slow Food officials visited Kenya when NECOFA (Network for Ecofarming in Africa) and other civil society organizations in Kenya were working hard to 'halt' and 'reverse' the process of erosion of indigenous cultures. Terra Madre 2004 and 2006 contributed significantly to this struggle. Kenyan food communities participated and interacted with others from all over the world that treasure and guard their food cultures jealously. The experience greatly reinforced the Kenyan communities' resolve to reclaim the eroded 'glory' of their indigenous food cultures and augmented their confidence and pride in their communities.

The Kenyan representatives went even further, establishing the Kenya Terra Madre Coordinating Committee to coordinate Slow Food membership recruitment, set up convivia and promote networking and collaboration among food communities and convivia. The strength of Slow Food in Kenya is thus founded on collaboration and information sharing and exchange. While Kenya and Africa generally are still lagging behind in terms of 'modern' information and communication technology, our communities are committed to sharing information with others. Exchange visits arranged among food communities to encourage interaction have more than one benefit. Besides offering a chance to exchange information on food and economic empowerment, they also provide an opportunity for making merry, singing and dancing, swapping and sharing planting materials, and bartering and trading food.

After Terra Madre 2006, chefs were 'looped' into the network and this boosted the membership and the impact of the network itself. Its interactions and activities have forged a 'brotherhood' of food communities, now more than ever concerned about the welfare and wellbeing of each other. In October 2007, the members and the food communities of the Central Rift Convivium contributed foodstuffs that they delivered to the community of Longicharo in the arid Baringo district. Another demonstration of 'brotherhood' is the positive action taken by members of oth-

THE STRENGTH OF SLOW FOOD IN KENYA IS FOUNDED ON COLLABORATION
AND INFORMATION SHARING AND EXCHANGE BETWEEN COMMUNITIES AND CONVIVIA.

SOLIDARITY

er convivia and food communities towards Internally Displaced Persons (IDPs) in the Central Rift Valley following the post-election violence that hit many parts of Kenya. The Central Rift was one of the 'trouble spots' and even Slow Food members and food communities suffered great losses.

schools and is now being replicated in others within other convivia. This replication or broadening out of 'good practices' is another important virtue of Terra Madre networking in Kenya. The Central Rift learned from the Western Kenya Convivium how to organize competitions on indigenous foods, with young people

CONVIVIA
FOOD COMMUNITIES

SCHOOL GARDENS

In collaboration with NECOFA and Friends of Kenya Schools and Wildlife (FKSW), the Central Rift Convivum has initiated school garden projects in several schools since 2006. The initiative is aimed at inculcating positive values on food, agriculture and the environment in school youth. Objectives of the initiative include: training young people for a future as food producers and/or co-producers; providing hands-on experience; using school gardens as training/learning centers for the community; multiplying and bulking planting materials and small livestock for the community; involving young people in sensitizing the community on management of the environment and biodiversity; building the capacity of young people and the community to access and share information; teaching young people teamwork and leadership skills.

The initiative has proved successful in six

preparing and presenting meals and elderly men and women judging them. Most of these 'good practices' are shared and learned during food fairs and events in which convivium food community members participate.

Networking is also boosted by the partnerships developed among food producers and cooks at food outlets. These have also significantly improved the income of individual members and convivia.

The communities' desire and urge for more knowledge has grown insatiable, and in December 2007 28 of them traveled to neighboring Uganda for interaction and information sharing with communities there. The initiative reinforced ties among communities, with the Ugandans sending food and support to Kenyans affected by the post-electoral violence. In conclusion, the Terra Madre network is continuing to grow in Kenya and beyond.

FOTO M. MESMAIN

THE SCHOOL GARDENS PROJECT GOES BEYOND ITS EDUCATIONAL OBJECTIVE TO INVOLVE STUDENTS, PARENTS AND TEACHERS. IT IS THE FIRST STEP TOWARDS CREATING A LEARNING COMMUNITY

LEARNING TOGETHER

Cristina Bertazzoni
Italy, educator and lecturer in Education Technologies and Techniques at the University of Brescia

NETWORK

The Italian 'Orto in Condotta' School Gardens project does more than merely design and create eco-friendly gardens for students and teachers. As Slow Food has stated more than once in documents on the subject, the project seeks to develop and promote local 'learning communities'. What is the significance of this concept? What educational reference points have inspired the idea of community learning? To answer these questions we must set out from the term 'learning community' and try to understand their deeper meanings. As the distinguished psychoanalyst Franco Fornari has shown, the word 'community' has a dual semantic value, deriving from *cum munus* (gift) and *cum moenia* (wall, bulwark).

The concept of community thus combines the idea of a gift, an unconditional exchange, with the defensive logic of an encircling wall marking a territory and protecting it from outside attacks. Central to the term *community* is thus the idea of meetings among people who exchange gifts and who, at the same time, share a common identity and a circumscribed territory distinct from others.

KNOWLEDGE EXCHANGE

Slow Food genuinely interprets this double meaning: the School Gardens project is a tool, a catalyst of relationships among people—grandparents with kitchen gardens, teachers, students, families, citizens, public authorities, convivium committees, local producers—who, by sharing the experience of the garden, exchange intangible gifts, namely knowledge and skills, and thus weave a dynamic, vital cooperative fabric. At the same time, this community of people becomes a collective for the defense of local agricultural and food culture. Local produce is cultivated in the garden using organic methods and with a special eye to

THE SCHOOL
GARDEN PROJECT

crops at risk of extinction. As recipes, traditions, family stories and tales of farming are recounted and passed on, so the memory, identity and distinctive features of the local area are preserved. This kind of community, as understood by Slow Food, is focused on learning. It is not just a web of relationships structured around an initiative/stimulus (*the garden*), but also an educational community, a space in which people teach and learn. The concept of 'learning' correlated to 'community' emphasizes a conception of learning not just as a simple passage of information from someone who knows to someone who doesn't, according to a vision of the mind as an empty vessel waiting to be filled. Learning is instead understood as a constructive process that occurs within and through relationships, knowledge exchange, experience sharing and the construction of the significances to attribute to what we do together and what we tell each other.

INDIVIDUALS

Learning is not an intra-individual event but a social, community process. As Lev Vygotsky has said, 'The interpsychic becomes intrapsychic': the growth of cultural knowledge and skills has a collective matrix (interpsychic). These social experiences become the property of the individual (intrapsychic) who belongs to that socio-cultural context. The concept of a learning community contains within itself this complexity, to which is connected a strong tendency towards change. To promote a learning community in fact means encouraging an action with a high transformative potential. The intention is to change the behavior, attitudes and awareness towards our daily diet, agriculture, the protection of local products and cuisine, and in general to promote a renewed relationship with food culture in all its aspects (production, gastronomy, consumption). Taking action in an area in order to realize a learning community project therefore means activating a process of relationship and exchange among groups such as parents, students and producers. As the psychology of communities teaches us, it is a process based on the 'strategy of connections'. The School Gardens project is one of the actions that aims to transform an archipelago of groups into a system, capable of working towards common goals and transforming itself into an educational community.

References
Bruner J., *La cultura dell'educazione*, Feltrinelli, Milan 1997.
Francescato D., Tomai M., Girelli G., *Fondamenti di psicologia di comunità*, Carocci, Rome 2002.
Vygotsky L. S., *Mind in Society. The Development of Higher Psychological processes*, Harvard University Press, Cambridge Mass. 1978.

THE PROJECT INTERCONNECTS GRANDPARENTS WITH KITCHEN GARDENS, TEACHERS, STUDENTS AND THEIR FAMILIES.

GARDENS IN LIGURIA

One of the first Italian examples of a learning community developing out of school gardens is the project put in place by nine municipal authorities, the Ingauna Mountain Community and 16 schools around Albenga in western Liguria. This land was inhabited by the Ingauni tribe before the Romans came, and it is here that the local people have come together to form a network and rediscover a sense of community.

Teachers and schoolchildren started by digging up the earth, working during school hours. At Villanova d'Albenga they had to remove all the stones from the soil before they could start sowing and planting. Each school made its own decisions about how to cultivate the gardens, some concentrating on typical local produce such as Albenga *trombetta* courgettes or Nasino *gianetti* beans, others following biodynamic principles.

At all the schools it was gratifying to see parents and the elderly getting involved in this new experience for the children, giving advice and helping manage the allotments. A team of 30 kitchen-gardener grandparents was formed with the task of passing on traditional farming wisdom to the younger generations. The teachers attended training courses, funded by the Mountain Community, to help them find the best ways to interweave the garden experience with other subjects.

The nine participating municipal authorities—all representing very small towns, from Ceriale's 5,000 inhabitants to Arnasco's 500 and Zuccarello's 300—chose to involve the whole population through a range of different initiatives, all aimed at giving value to the gardens as tools for food education and the protection and promotion of local culture. In this context, the success of the play entitled *Processo alle verdure* (Vegetables On Trial) and that of the great festival of Ingauni vegetables held in Garlenda at the end of May 2008, when over 1,000 green-fingered Ligurian schoolchildren met to play and eat together, came as no surprise.

ACQUA SPAREA

HAPPY HOUR   HAPPY WATER

SOPHISTICATED IN ITS FORMS, PURE AND SUBTLE IN ITS FLAVOUR, SPAREA
MINERAL WATER CAN ONLY BE FOUND IN THE BEST RESTAURANTS AND
MOST REFINED LOUNGES. IN THE RIGHT PLACE, AT THE RIGHT TIME.

THE SLOW FOOD IS MOVING FORWARD THANKS TO THE <mark>YOUTH FOOD MOVEMENT</mark>

Leaving A Mark

Elizabeth Manning
USA, coordinator of the Youth Food Movement

EDUCATION

In September 2007, students at Princeton University, New Jersey, enjoyed the new experience of speaking with producers while tasting and buying fresh seasonal produce at their first on-campus farmers' market. The market was organized by Kate and friends from the recently opened Princeton Convivium, one of eleven US Slow Food chapters run by college and tertiary students.

Meanwhile in Oregon, 24-year-old Alyssa and other young members of the local convivium are getting their hands dirty growing heirloom vegetables, providing fresh produce for the 55 families who back their Community Supported Agriculture farm. She wants to convince

her generation that there is nothing more intellectually stimulating, demanding of creativity or truly inspiring than farming.

Across the Pacific in Macau, a student convivium holds an event in the college hall, showcasing the diversity of local shellfish and mushroom varieties with the aim of reconnecting this modern Chinese city, built on gambling and tourism, with traditional food and a slow life.

In northern Italy, a group of international students from the University of Gastronomic Sciences ride their bikes along the River Po. Pedaling their way for 25 days, the students reflect on the past and future of food and how they can work to maintain healthy relationships between production, ecosystems, people and identity.

From Princeton to the Po, from the first campus convivium in Kenya to the inaugural Real Food Summit at Yale University, a movement is being born in all corners of the world. The young students and producers start to connect and become aware of a rise, worldwide, of youth eager to engage in Slow Food activities, while finding their own unique way to promote the philosophy.

PURE ENERGY

In October 2007, the movement was unified further when an international youth delegation of 18 students and producers traveled to the Fifth International Slow Food Congress in Puebla, Mexico. Having developed a joint proposal, the group took the stage and asked the gathered Slow Food representatives to support their ideas and projects. The Youth Food Movement was born to a standing ovation.

Today, the movement is developing in three key directions.

BRINGING 1,500 YOUNG PRODUCERS, COOKS AND STUDENTS FROM WIDELY DIVERSE PERSPECTIVES AND HOMELANDS TO THE 2008 MEETING IN TURIN IS A GREAT START TO ENERGIZING THIS GLOBAL EFFORT TOWARDS SUSTAINABLE FOOD PRODUCTION.

I) It is involving young people in the shaping of the future of food. Increasingly, food sustainability issues are capturing the attention of young food activists, who are organizing themselves to bring concrete change to our food system. In particular, higher education institutions provide an untapped potential for improving our food system through their course syllabuses, sustainable on-site food programs and student campaigns. The *Slow Food on Campus* program is growing rapidly across the US.

II) Young members of food communities are being connected through the Terra Madre network. Bringing 1,500 young producers, cooks and students from widely diverse perspectives and homelands to the 2008 meeting in Turin is a great start to energizing this global effort towards sustainable food production.

III) The movement is focusing on recovering wisdom by protecting, defending, reappraising and using traditional agricultural and artisan food production knowhow. Pangea is a new exchange program that places young apprentices with producers, who are exceptional stores of information, skills and knowledge. The project ensures the passing on of this knowledge through mentorship and encourages young people to become producers themselves.

The Youth Food Movement is at a very early stage of development. Like Slow Food, as it grows it will be open to various forms of interpretation and action by young people round the world. In the words of one member, Dave Schwartz from Brown University, 'It can be thought of as a moving train, with much weight behind it. Now, young people are the ones that have the ability to carry Slow Food into the new generation, into a new phase. There is so much energy, there is so much passion around young people in our country and throughout the world. This movement is an incredible opportunity both for young people and for Slow Food. It's an opportunity and it's also an invitation'.

Certified SA8000 by
BVQi

DE CECCO
E' UN'AZIENDA
CERTIFICATA
SA 8000

A guarantee of ethical practices.

De Cecco has attained Social Accountability certification (SA8000). A commitment to integrity.

We have always done our very best.

We have always taken the utmost care when choosing every ingredient in our products.

We have always devoted the same attention to the quality of the working environment and safeguarding the rights of our employees.

Now all of this is certified.

Recognition for our consistency and ethical principles.

di De Cecco ce n'è una sola.

WE ARE CONSCIOUSLY UPROOTING ANCIENT LOCAL VARIETIES OF FRUIT, VEGETABLES AND CEREALS, AND REPLACING TRADITIONAL BREEDS OF CATTLE, SHEEP AND PIGS WITH MODERN HYBRIDS.

IT IS THE ANIMAL AND PLANT SPECIES SKILLFULLY SELECTED BY HUMANS OVER
TIME WHICH ARE CURRENTLY MOST ENDANGERED. AND THE DESTRUCTION IS BEING
METHODICALLY PERPETRATED BY HUMANS THEMSELVES.

DOMESTIC
AND WILD

Piero Sardo
Italy, President of the Slow Food Foundation
for Biodiversity

BIODIVERSITY

For some time we have argued that Slow Food should be concerned with domestic biodiversity, because it is domestic biodiversity that provides most of our everyday food. Food is our specific area of interest: our association's purpose and strategies are based on agricultural issues, farming and food processing. To tell the truth, we have never considered whether this division of life on Earth into domestic and wild isn't somewhat arbitrary or vague. Academic science doesn't refer to the distinction, and when it analyses the effects of human impact on living nature, it is never concerned about which perspective it should be examined from. Whether it is a question of pollution, deforestation or agriculture, science studies the changes, or rather the damage, that human action has caused to the biosphere. It uses specialized approaches, maybe only looking at limited geographical areas, but without making a distinction between domestic and wild. There are some questions which need clarify-

ing. First of all, not all the food which human beings consume derives from agriculture and farming, the practices which historically have isolated useful species for domestication from biodiversity. Humans take plant food (mushrooms, herbs, berries, truffles) and animals (by hunting and fishing) from the wild habitat but, if we exclude fishing which requires separate consideration, it appears that the amounts involved are negligible. There are no exact data: the FAO provides detailed statistics on everything to do with food, but tells us nothing about plant food taken from the wild habitat. There probably aren't sufficient data to produce reliable statistical information and, in any case, it would seem that the activity of gatherers does not constitute a serious threat to biodiversity.

INDIRECT THREAT
Hunting and fishing are something else. They are carefully monitored because the catching of excessive amounts is reducing natural

THE COEXISTENCE OF WILD AND DOMESTIC BIODIVERSITY ASSURED THE VIGOR OF THE SOIL, THE PRESENCE OF ANIMALS CAPABLE OF ATTACKING HARMFUL INSECTS, AND VARIABILITY INSIDE SPECIES.

resources down to the levels essential for survival. In fact, in many countries hunting is strictly regulated, and raised species are being released into the natural habitat in order to maintain biodiversity at levels that allow people to practice recreational hunting. The latter is still a widespread activity, but marginal in terms of providing food—people hunt for sport—and will only survive, at least in developed countries, if assisted. With fishing it is the increasing demand for fish as a food that is putting pressure on natural resources to the very limits of sustainability. The 'domestic' alternative of fish farming presents a series of problems (environmental, technological, health) that do not at present allow us to replace wild fishing. On account of its specific characteristics, which are bound to to global eating habits, Slow Food classifies fishing as similar to domestic biodiversity, even if this does not strictly correspond to truth. But if we ask a second question, we can see there is partial justification for this arbitrary classification. For some decades human beings have consciously and methodically attacked domestic biodiversity in order to reduce, simplify and standardize it. However indirect threats to wild biodiversity are, they are an effect of our increasingly mindless exploitation of the planet: nobody wants to intentionally cause the extinction of butterflies, pandas, Bengal tigers, holm oaks or the rainforest. Human beings are endangering them because they are digging wells, cultivating virgin land, releasing chemical substances into the soil, artificially increasing the fertility of crops, exhausting water resources, changing the climate, removing natural habitats and modifying ecological communities. We are not intentionally putting species at risk. Instead we are consciously uprooting ancient local varieties of fruit, vegetables and cereals, and replacing traditional breeds of cattle, sheep and pigs with modern hybrids. It is a worldwide attack on the wealth of countries and the knowledge of people, allegedly carried out to rationalize herbs and crops to achieve greater profitability. What human beings have knowledgeably and patiently selected over 10,000 years, conjuring up extraordinary biodiversity from nothing, is now being progressively eliminated by human beings. It might be objected that the few thousand species selected by humans that are now at risk of extinction, constitute a tiny proportion of biodiversity compared to the total. In fact it is estimated that the number of species existing today is much greater than the 1,400,000 officially classified. In her *The Work of Nature*, Yvonne Baskin speaks of 30 million species, though a number between 10 and 15 million is probably more realistic. These numbers are so high they make one wonder whether the end of the Burlina cow or criollo corn is no more than a whisper in the deafening concert of life on Earth.

ZERO LEVEL

It's true that, thousands of years ago, agriculture and livestock farming began to sim-

HOWEVER INDIRECT THREATS TO WILD BIODIVERSITY ARE, THEY ARE AN EFFECT OF OUR INCREASINGLY MINDLESS EXPLOITATION OF THE PLANET.

AND WILD
DOMESTIC

plify the human diet somehat. When humans were hunters and gatherers—some people maintain this was the true golden age of *Homo sapiens*—they obtained nutrition from at least 8,000 plant species. Sedentarization progressively reduced this range to the current 150 species, of which five provide 50 percent of food needs. But now interspecies biodiversity, variability and the ability created by evolution to multiply differences to ensure better defense against pathogens and disease are also seriously threatened. The monocultures promoted by agroindustry—controlled and without interspecies differences—represent zero level biodiversity. Yet this method of farming is universally applied in the name of greater productivity, with chemical substances being used to make up for the fragility of these simplified species. Monocultures require extensive areas of land to eliminate obstacles: they mean the end of hedgerows, trees, mixed crops, rotation, fallow land and soil vitality. They mean removing anything that does not assure maximum efficiency and income—meaning traditional breeds and species.

This attack on biodiversity is also being launched at sea. Fishermen know that they are seriously depleting resources, that there is excessive pressure on some species. But they continue to fish because the world fishing system is demanding greater availability and guarantees ever growing markets. The context is obviously differ-ent: in the oceans the attack on marine biodiversity risks being fatal and definitive, whereas on land its effects are partial and quantitatively non-relevant, as we have seen. It is the implications that are different and much more worrying. By eliminating domestic biodiversity, we inflict a fatal attack on local cultures and historic habitats, where the interaction between local species and wild biodiversity had been consolidated and tested over centuries of agricultural practice. The coexistence of wild and domestic biodiversity was necessary: it assured the vigor of the soil, the presence of animals capable of attacking harmful insects, variability inside species, the vitality of the landscape, and natural productive processes.

It is no coincidence that the organic methods now desirable for agriculture were general practice only 50 years ago, maybe less. And while the disappearance of local crops in rich countries means the loss of values and traditions but not poverty, in poor countries it has led to the total loss of food sovereignty which, with ongoing food price increases, risks degenerating into a frightening food tragedy. Slow Food is developing its activities on these two fronts, defending traditions in developed countries to preserve local identities, wholesome produce and the pleasure of eating, and preserving local economies in poorer countries as their only defense against hunger and the food crisis.

Bottega Vinai. La linea che tutti ci invidiano.

www.cavit.it

Tappo rigorosamente in sughero

Silhouette slanciata, veste elegante

Denominazione di origine controllata

Segno di appartenenza

Colori morbidi ma decisi

BOTTEGA VINAI

TRENTINO
MÜLLER THURGAU
V.Q.P.R.D.

CAVIT

BOTTEGA VINAI

TRENTINO
MARZEMINO

BOTTEGA VINAI

TRAMINER
AROMATICO

CAVIT
TRENTO

Non c'è solo l'elegante silhouette e il look inconfondibile dietro al successo di Bottega Vinai. C'è il rigore, la passione e l'impegno di una vita. C'è il desiderio di esprimere in 13 vini, ottenuti da vigneti di eccellenza, la grande vocazione enologica del Trentino. Scegliendo Bottega Vinai saprete di aver scelto il meglio.

CHARDONNAY ▸ MÜLLER THURGAU ▸ NOSIOLA ▸ PINOT GRIGIO ▸ SAUVIGNON ▸ TRAMINER ▸ SCHIAVA GENTILE ▸ CABERNET SAUVIGNON ▸ LAGREIN DUNKEL ▸ MARZEMINO ▸ MERLOT ▸ PINOT NERO ▸ TEROLDEGO

NEI MIGLIORI RISTORANTI, ENOTECHE E WINE BAR. BOTTEGA VINAI, TRENTO E LODE

DOES CLIMATE CHAOS SPELL AN END TO AGRICULTURAL BIODIVERSITY? FOR THE MULTINATIONALS, THE ONLY SOLUTION IS TO PATENT SEEDS. BUT SMALL FARMERS DON'T AGREE. AND THEY'RE NOT THE ONLY ONES.

FOOD SOVEREIGNTY

Pat Roy Mooney
Canada, executive director of the ETC
(Erosion, Technology and Concentration) Group

BIODIVERSITY

When a human-made food emergency meets a human-made climate crisis, the effect on humanity is rather like sitting a cyclone on top of a tsunami. And, between the cyclone and the tsunami, most of the world's remaining agricultural biodiversity may blow away.

Recent climate-crop analyses suggest that the hottest five years of the 20th century may match the coldest five years at the end of this century. From Nepal to Ethiopia to Bolivia, farmers and their crops and livestock will encounter temperatures they've never seen before and no one can be sure whether the chickpeas or the chickens will survive. Tragically, the traditional farmer-bred seeds and breeds and their wild relatives on the fringes and in the forests—with the very genetic diversity the planet needs to adjust to climate change—may also disappear.

SEED AGAINST SEED

Multinational seed companies, the top 10 of whom control 57 percent of global commercial seed sales, are betting that their patented varieties, engineered for sales over the widest possible land area and growing conditions, will be more 'climate-ready' than farmer-bred varieties especially developed for the microclimate of a specific farming community. Conversely, peasant producers insist that large-scale industrial farms will be the ones in trouble and contend that their own seeds have the built-in resilience and robustness to adjust to rapidly changing climates, pests, and diseases. Not only are farmers' varieties tough and diverse, peasants argue, but small farmers plant more crops and more varieties within each crop. Who's right? The companies, at least, see this as a 'winner-takes-all' debate. We either opt for industrial agriculture or for what farmers are calling 'Food Sovereignty'. Companies like Monsanto, BASF, DuPont, Syngenta and Dow have ways of hedging their bets. Under pressure from bilateral, regional and WTO trade negotiations, national governments in the global South are adopting seed laws related to nomenclature, variety maintenance, uniformity and market rules

AGRICULTURAL BIODIVERSITY

that are already driving local agricultural biodiversity into extinction. Patent laws and licenses are making it almost impossible for farmers to save or exchange their own seeds. In the midst of climate chaos when we need all the diversity we can get, corporations are winning the commercial battle to destroy the diversity.

PATENT FAMILIES

If wiping out the competition weren't enough, the companies are also positioning themselves to profit from the climate-induced crop uncertainties ahead. In the last few years, the largest biotech seed companies have applied or received more than 500 patents they claim will help crops respond to a wide-range of stresses—from heat or cold tolerance to salt and flood tolerance. These patents are remarkable. Many of them individually cover many—or all—of the world's crops; most or all forms of trees; and claim gigantic gene sequences they have not invented but found. BASF's patent, US No. 7,161,063, for instance, claims a sequence associated with increased tolerance to environmental stress found in any transgenic 'maize, wheat, rye, oat, triticale, rice, barley, soybean, peanut, cotton, rapeseed, canola, manihot, pepper, sunflower, tagetes, solanaceous plants, potato, tobacco, eggplant, tomato, *Vicia* species, pea, alfalfa, coffee, cacao, tea, *Salix* species, oil palm, coconut, perennial grass and a forage crop plant'.[1] Try to get through the day without eating one of these!

The monopoly is tighter than even this suggests. The 500-plus patents actually merge into 55 of what patent offices call 'families' 51 of these 55 'cosa nostras' are held by six agribusiness giants: BASF, Bayer, Dow, DuPont, Monsanto and Syngenta—or small, specialty biotech companies partnering with the big corporations. BASF itself has 21 'families' but has established a joint venture with Monsanto which directly holds another six and, indirectly, has interests in companies that hold a further nine. In other words, BASF and Monsanto together directly hold 27 and, indirectly, 36 of the 55 critical patent families.

BIOFUEL CYCLONE

The six companies, of course, argue that farmers—and the competition—don't need to buy or mimic their products. Yet these six companies together control 73 percent of world pesticide sales and four of them have more than 40 percent of global seed sales. Where they go—others must follow. Already, leading public-sector researchers including the 15 institutes of the Consultative Group on International Agricultural Research (CGIAR, the Green Revolution folks)—are indicating that 'climate-ready' gene sequences and GE technologies may be the best response to climate change.

In fact, some of the leading scientists within the CGIAR paint an extraordinarily pessimistic picture of the future of peasant agriculture. They assume a relatively rapid 'tipping' in crop climatic conditions that will

MULTINATIONAL SEED COMPANIES ARE BETTING THAT THEIR PATENTED VARIETIES WILL BE MORE 'CLIMATE-READY' THAN FARMER-BRED VARIETIES.

AGRICULTURAL BIODIVERSITY

oblige agricultural scientists to focus on the major crops (wheat, rice, maize, potatoes, soybeans) in the major growing areas—the Plains, Prairies, Pampas and Punjab. That means that the 1.4 billion people living in rural areas who depend upon farmer-saved seed and live on marginal lands will have to make their way to the cities. To this glum prediction, the big biotech companies add that the abandoned hillsides can then be converted to agrifuel production. These companies are working closely with Big Oil and food processors to develop 'Generation 2' agrofuels that can turn cellulosic fiber into liquid fuel and specialty chemicals—the long awaited 'carbohydrate economy'. The agrofuels market is expected to jump from $22 billion in $2006 to $150 billion around 2020. In 2006, less than 2 percent of the world's arable land was sown to fuel crops. By around 2020 fuel crop's share will rise to 12 percent. Agrofuel's pressure on our land resources is also fueling a hike in food prices. In 2004, the global grocery bill stood at $5.5 trillion but, by 2009, industry analysts say it will top $8.5 trillion. This is where the cyclone of agrofuels meets the tsunami of climate chaos.

VIA CAMPESINA

As quickly as farmers blow into the cities, agricultural biodiversity will blow into history. Between big biotech's transgenically uniform crops in the most favored growing regions and the spread of equally-uniform fuel crops in harsher terrains, the crop seeds that have been nurtured by farm families for 12,000 years will become extinct.

Is there a realistic alternative? Absolutely. The Via Campesina—the world's largest network of small farmers—has joined forces with pastoralists, fisherfolk and indigenous peoples to promote a much more holistic view of food and agriculture within the framework of Food Sovereignty. The concept emphasizes local production and consumption and fairness toward both producers and consumers. Food Sovereignty also treasures genetic diversity. Rather than adopt an untested and monopolistic high-tech approach to climate change, small farmers are pressing for the development of 'underutilized' crops that have shown their enormous plasticity in the face of changing conditions as well as considerable nutritional qualities. Two decades ago, in an unfortunately titled series describing the 'Lost Crops' of Africa and the Andes, the US National Research Council called for the development of more than 50 crops that seem to have adaptability to temperature, sunlight, altitude, and precipitation that make excellent candidates for further exploration. The 50 crops are almost never found in national or global gene banks and are only protected today in farmers' fields. If we can work with the world's small farmers to develop this diversity, maybe our children won't be left biting the dust.

Note
1. A world map published by ETC Group and USC Canada is available in English, French, and Spanish, titled 'The Seed Map'. It can be downloaded at www.seedmap.org.

CRUSHED BY BIG BIOTECH'S TRANSGENICALLY UNIFORM CROPS, THE CROP SEEDS THAT HAVE BEEN NURTURED BY FARM FAMILIES FOR 12,000 YEARS WILL BECOME EXTINCT.

CROPS AND CLIMATE CHAOS – POINTS TO PONDER

- A temperature increase of 3-4°C could cause crop yields to fall by 15-35 percent in Africa and west Asia and by 25-35 percent in the Middle East according to an FAO report released in March 2008.[1]
- 65 countries in the South, most in Africa, risk losing 280 million tons of potential cereal production, valued at $56 billion, as a result of climate change. [2]
- Projected increases in temperature and changes in rainfall patterns will decrease growing periods by more than 20 percent in many parts of sub-Saharan Africa. The most vulnerable communities across Africa are farming families in East and Central Africa, including Rwanda, Burundi, Eritrea, and Ethiopia as well as Chad and Niger.[3]
- Farmers in dryland areas of sub-Saharan Africa will experience revenue losses of 25 percent per acre by 2060. The overall revenue losses of $26 billion per annum would exceed current levels of bilateral aid to the region. [4]
- Asian rice yields will decrease dramatically due to higher night-time temperatures. With warmer conditions, photosynthesis slows or ceases, pollination is prevented, and dehydration sets in. A study by the International Rice Research Institute reports that rice yields are declining by 10 percent for every degree Celsius increase in night-time temperatures. [5]
- South Asia's prime wheat-growing land—the vast Indo-Gangetic plain which produces about 15 percent of the world's wheat crop—will shrink 51 percent by 2050 due to hotter, drier weather and diminished yields, a loss that will place at least 200 million people at greater risk of hunger.[6]
- Latin America and Africa and will see a 10 percent decline in maize productivity by 2055—equivalent to crop losses worth US $2 billion per year.[7]

- In Latin America, losses for rain-fed maize production will be far higher than for irrigated production; some models predict losses of up to 60 percent for Mexico, where around 2 million smallholder farmers depend on rain-fed maize cultivation.[8]
- Wild crop relatives will be particularly vulnerable to extinction due to climate change. A study of wild plant species related to food crops estimates that 16-22 percent of the wild relatives of cowpea, peanut and potato will become extinct by 2055 and the geographic range of the remaining wild species will be reduced by more than half.[9] Crop wild relatives are a vital source of resistance genes for future crop improvement, but their habitat is threatened and only a small percentage of these species is held in gene bank collections.
- Over a much longer time scale, 2070-2100, climate models predict extreme climatic changes and unthinkable projections for food security: During the last three decades of this century, the mean temperature in many of the world's poorest countries will surpass what the same countries experienced as the most extreme warm temperatures between 1900-2000. In other words, models predict that the coolest temperatures experienced during growing seasons in 2070-2100 will be warmer than the hottest growing seasons observed over the past century. In India, for example, between 1900-2000 the mean growing season temperatures hovered between 26 and 28°C; between 2070-2100 the mean growing season temperatures are projected to be approximately 29-30°. In Kenya, the mean growing season temperatures in the last century were approximately 21-22° C; climate scientists predict Kenya's mean growing season temperatures at the end of this century (2070-2100) will hover around 23-25°C.

Note
1. FAO, Press Release, 'Agriculture in the Near East likely to suffer from climate change', Rome/Cairo, March 3 2008. http://www.fao.org/newsroom/en/news/2008/1000800/index.html
2. United Nations News Centre, FAO, 'Climate change threatens crop losses, more hungry people – UN,' May 26 2005.
3. Thornton P.K, et al., *Mapping Climate Vulnerability and Poverty in Africa*, International Livestock Research Institute, May 2006. The report finds that many communities across Africa that are already grappling with severe poverty are also at the cross-hairs of the most adverse effects of climate change. Most vulnerable of all are farming families in East and Central Africa, including Rwanda, Burundi, Eritrea, and Ethiopia as well as Chad and Niger. http://www.ilri.org/ILRIPubAware/Uploadedpercent20Files/Mapping percent20Climate percent20Vulnerability percent20and percent20Poverty percent20in percent20Africa.pdf
4. UNDP, *Human Development Report 2007/2008*, p. 92.
5. IRRI, Press Release, 'Rice harvests more affected than first thought by global warming,' 29 June 2004. The study was published in Proceedings of the National Academy of Sciences.
6. Consultative Group on International Agricultural Research, News Release, 'Intensified Research Effort Yields Climate-Resilient Agriculture To Blunt Impact of Global Warming, Prevent Widespread Hunger,' December 4 2006. The title of the forthcoming study is, 'Can Wheat Beat the Heat?' On the Internet: http://www.cgiar.org/pdf/agm06/AGM06 percent20Press percent20Release percent20FINAL.pdf
7. CGIAR, 'Global Climate Change: Can Agriculture Cope?' Online Briefing Dossier, 2007. On the Internet: http://www.cgiar.org/impact/global/cc_mappingthemenace.html
8. UNDP, *Human Development Report 2007/2008*, p. 94.
9. CGIAR, 'Global Climate Change: Can Agriculture Cope?' Online Briefing Dossier, 2007. On the Internet: http://www.cgiar.org/impact/global/cc_mappingthemenace.html

1984 REVOLUTION

NINETEEN-EIGHTY-FOUR WAS A LANDMARK YEAR FOR DUCA DI SALAPARUTA AND THE WORLD OF WINE PRODUCTION. IT WAS THE YEAR OF THE ARRIVAL OF DUCA ENRICO, A GREAT ARISTOCRATIC RED, MADE FROM THE NERO D'AVOLA GRAPE AND AN INTENSE EXPRESSION OF ITS TERRORY.

TWO-THOUSAND-NINE. IN 25 YEARS DUCA ENRICO HAS, YEAR ON YEAR, WON THE MOST PRESTIGIOUS INTERNATIONAL PRIZES AND AWARD, AND HAS BEEN CONFIRMED AS AN AUTHENTIC SYMBOL OF ITALIAN WINE CULTURE THROUGHOUT THE WORDL.

DUCA DI SALAPARUTA

DAL 1824

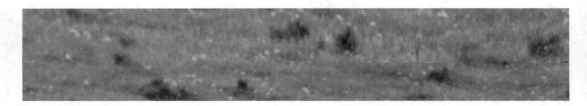

THE TERM PRESIDIUM IS NOT ALWAYS A SYNONYM FOR 'TRADITIONAL PRODUCT'. TO ASSURE A FUTURE FOR A LOCAL COMMUNITY IN TIBET, SLOW FOOD DECIDED TO CREATE A CHEESE WHICH DID NOT EXIST BUT COULD ENHANCE THE AREA'S RESOURCES.

THE RIGHT RECIPE

Serena Milano
Italy, director of the Slow Food Foundation
for Biodiversity
Photos Paola Vanzo

A peaceful people with their own language and culture and an intrinsically non-violent religion has suffered all sorts of aggression for decades. The most dangerous effects are internal and moral: the fact that crowds of the young and the not so young, monks and civilians react from time to time with futile protests that meet ruthless repression might surprise us westerners, so obsessed with rational calculations, opportunism and realpolitik. But we should ask whether these uprisings, regularly suppressed with bloodshed, don't represent something more profound than an expression of desperation, something nobler than an understandable human exasperation ... I believe they are a strong affirmation of a 'another' way of life, a diversity which refuses to accept that it is going to disappear ... The Tibetan monks rise in revolt to stress that there is 'something to live for, something important enough to die for', they demonstrate because they feel a deep-seated need for justice, no matter how unlikely they are to obtain the justice they ask for.

Enzo Bianchi, prior of the Bose monastic community, Piedmont, Italy
La Stampa, 20/03/2008

BIODIVERSITY

'It is now more important than ever to continue supporting this project,' writes Paola Vanzo, spokesperson of the American Trace Foundation and coordinator of the Tibetan Yak Cheese Presidium. Her email arrived in April, little more than a month after the protests and hundreds of deaths in Tibet. Paola had just managed to contact Gyaltsen from the United States: 'I am glad to report that Jigme Gyaltsen and all his community are well,' she added. That was the news we were hoping to hear.

SPIRITUALITY AND YAKS

Jigme Gyaltsen is the monk we are now accustomed to seeing wearing his purplish red robes and a seraphic smile, behind his Presidium's stand at the Cheese or Salone del

TIBET
SPIRITUALITY AND YAKS

Gusto events, intent on slicing yak cheese and offering samples to anyone nearby. But in the Ragya monastery in Qinghai, he is a moral, spiritual and political authority.

In 1994 he founded a private school bearing his name and offering free education to 600 Tibetan children, sons and daughters of nomadic families. It is the only school which, in addition to modern education, also adopts millenary methods, such as philological debate for teaching the sciences.

For ten years the school kept going thanks to public and private donations and the support of the Trace Foundation, which funded courses, classrooms, laboratories, a canteen and salaries for teachers. Then Gyaltsen decided to undertake an activity that would finance the school, at least partly, and at the same time preserve the nomadic culture. The activity involved the symbolic animal of these high places, the yak, built to survive the harsh life of the Tibetan plateau, where, with the temperature sometimes plummeting to -30°C, it has to dig for the grass that lies buried for months under the snow.

The yak is an ungainly animal with a long thick coat which supplies the raw materials for all the herders' routine activities: hide and wool for clothing and tents, meat, milk and dung, which when dried is used as fuel. Families travel dozens of kilometers with their herds and everything they need to survive along difficult routes of dirt tracks, fords and vertical cliffs, to their summer pastures. The women, who deal with everything from tents to children to animals, milk the yaks twice a day, squatting beside the gentle giants in their loose skirts, held up by belts bedecked with medallions and pendants, and tall felt hats, their long thinly plaited jet-black hair framing their oval faces. Milk from the *dri* (the female yak) is consumed fresh or made into yogurt or butter. Boiled dried whey is used to make *chura*, one of the ingredients of the Tibetan breakfast, along with *tsampa* (roasted barley flour) and milky tea.

CHEESEMAKERS AT 4500 METERS

Local traditions do not envisage cheese at all, never mind mature cheese. In order to enable nomadic herders to earn a livelihood, the only possible solution was to produce a new cheese that would express the unique qualities of these grasslands and suitable for being kept long enough to be transported to western markets. Since Presidia promote local historic and traditional products, we initially reckoned it would be unthinkable to help produce and promote this type of cheese would not be possible. But the ethical value of the proposal put forward by Trace Foundation prevailed over theoretical correctness: after all, people sometimes die by sticking too rigidly to the rules, while even a small additional income for such disadvantaged populations can change their lives completely.

It was thus that in 2004 the Presidium for Tibetan yak cheese was created and the collaboration between the Slow Food Foundation

THE WOMEN, WHO DEAL WITH EVERYTHING FROM TENTS TO CHILDREN TO ANIMALS, MILK THE YAKS TWICE A DAY.

THE MILK IS PROCESSED TWICE A DAY AND HEATED IN COPPER POTS ON AN OPEN FIRE FUELLED BY DRY YAK DUNG.

for Biodiversity, the Trace Foundation and Ragya monastery got underway. A year later the three partners were joined by AVEC-PVS, an association of veterinarians, agronomists and cheese technicians who mainly work on issues involving products of animal origin and in the training sector. Helped by funding from the Val d'Aosta Regional Authority, the

hard paste and distinctive flavor, vaguely redolent of a good pecorino. It is a slowly aged cheese that begins to express its qualities after six months of aging. When cut, the paste is a dark straw color or yellow, depending on the forage eaten by the animals. The flavor and aroma are intense and full-bodied, with a prevalence of milk and herb sensations in

THE RIGHT RECIPE

association has since focused on milk hygiene and animal health.

For several summers some veterinarians and dairy technicians (Massimo Mercandino, Massimo Nurisso and Andrea Dominici of AVEC, Andrea Adami of ONAF and Swiss cheesemaker Ernst Holenstein) have spent several weeks on the Tibetan plateau at 4,500 meters in the monks' small cheesemaking facility at the intersection of three magnificent valleys where the yaks graze. The milk brought to the facility by 35 nomads is processed twice a day and heated in copper pots on an open fire fuelled by dry yak dung. About twelve Tibetans have worked with the AVEC experts, learning various cheesemaking methods.

After countless experiments the right recipe was found: a skimmed milk cheese with semi-

fresh cheeses and more developed notes of aromatic herbs, walnut and roasted hazelnut in aged ones.

The Presidium now has to find a market for its cheese. A complete ban on imports into Europe of any dairy produce made in China has made the promotional efforts and commercial support a much more difficult undertaking than Slow Food originally. But the process is now underway and, after various trials and errors, the cheeses are being aged, and the herders and monks hold out high expectations for them.

It would be small-minded and uncharitable to stop here. We need to promote widespread support and participation for the project, particularly in the United States where it is possible to export the cheese.

IN 2002, TWO COFFEE PRESIDIA WERE SET UP IN CENTRAL AMERICA, ALONG WITH A PROJECT FOR THE DIRECT SALE OF COFFEE TO LOCAL ROASTERS. THESE IDEAS HAVE BROUGHT IMPROVEMENTS TO COMMUNITY LIFE.

AROMAS IN A GLOBAL WORLD

Mariana Guimarães Weiler
Brazil, chief of Slow Food Foundation for Biodiversity activities in Latin America
Photos Alberto Peroli

BIODIVERSITÀ

On the wooden table are plates laden with turkey and spicy sauce, accompanied by rice, *tamales* (boiled cornmeal dough wrapped in the plant's leaves) and *tortillas* (corn pancakes), all served with delicately worked steel forks and spoons. In front of us is a spread of Guatemalan gastronomy, food for special occasions which has been prepared by our host, *dueña* Lucía Matías, to welcome European and American coffee roasters to Todos Santos. In this village hidden among the Huehuetenango mountains, the heat is a as fierce as the spicy condiment and I ask for a glass of water. The answer is evident in the wide-open, helpless eyes of our host. I feel uncomfortable: I could have been more sensitive, looked around and seen the glasses printed with the logos of international beverages and filled with an artificially flavored red liquid. Due to the serious pollution affecting

the quality of water resources, drinking water is rare in these parts.

WALL STREET AND COYOTES
Only when you see the everyday routine of the producers of the Huehuetenango Highlands Coffee Presidium can you understand the lives behind the coffee beans that arrive in European and North American ports. During our journey, undertaken in the company of five Italian coffee roasters, two Americans and one Dane, we see what it means to drive along dirt roads and negotiate steep slopes to reach the *cafetales*, the coffee plantations. We also realize how hard it is to survive a system controlled by and adapted for large companies: the costly certification processes and the difficulty in promoting the product on the global market were issues we discussed among the cof-

CENTRAL AMERICA
SMALL PRODUCERS

fee plants, which some roasters were seeing for the first time.

Coffee is a global product and its production and commercialization spread across three continents, directly or indirectly involving the work of millions of people from plantation to cup. The prices fixed by the exchanges in New York and London determine the fate of small farmers from Guatemala to India. Unfortunately, the commercialization system it controls is far from fair. Small farmers, who do not possess suitable equipment to transport their product from remote plantations to centers of trade, are forced to rely on *coyotes*, speculators who take advantage of the system to underpay farmers and then resell the goods loaded onto their pickup trucks.

A NETWORK OF SMALL PRODUCERS

Our journey was organized as part of the Café y Caffé project, which aims to create a network of small production cooperatives in Central America. The project is coordinated by the Istituto Agronomico per l'Oltremare (Overseas Agricultural Institute), with operational support from the Slow Food Foundation for Biodiversity and the Tuscan NGO UCODEP. The network of small Central American coffee producers, a sign of a new approach in a global world, is already a valuable instrument for exchanging know-how and information about good practices. At present six countries are benefiting from

ONLY WHEN YOU SEE THE EVERYDAY ROUTINE OF HUEHUETENANGO PRESIDIUM PRODUCERS CAN YOU UNDERSTAND THE LIVES BEHIND THE COFFEE BEANS THAT ARRIVE IN EUROPEAN AND NORTH AMERICAN PORTS.

CENTRAL AMERICA
COFFEE

the project: Guatemala, the Dominican Republic, Costa Rica, Salvador, Nicaragua and Honduras. The aim is to involve about 2,000 small producers and promote technology and information exchanges in a network for at least 30 bodies or organizations.

The initiative is making use of Slow Food's experience with its coffee presidia in Guatemala (Huehuetenango Highlands) and the Dominican Republic (Sierra Cafetalera), whose communities were the first to join the network. The Huehuetenango Presidium, set up in 2002, has already achieved a great deal. It now involves 160 small producers, who cultivate high-quality coffee at altitudes of over 1,500 meters. To ensure high standards of quality, the producers were helped by industry experts to draw up a set of production rules to guarantee not only excellent sensory characteristics but also environmental sustainability and a better life for people whose livelihood depends on coffee. The production rules are an example for other cooperatives in the network and, adapted to each particular situation, will interconnect the small Central American producers. The small producers in the network will stand out for the quality of their coffee, the only real form of differentiation on the global market.

A SHORT SUPPLY CHAIN

Presidium coffee was also the object of a roasting project launched in 2005 in Turin's Vallette prison by the Pausa Café social cooperative. Since then a group of prisoners has learned the art of traditional wood-fired roasting using presidium coffee from Guatemala and the Dominican Republic, purchased at a fair and profitable price. The Guatemalan producers are members of the cooperative and every year receive 50 percent of the profits, thereby benefiting from the later stages of coffee production which account for most of the added value.

From the presidium's earliest beginnings, finding direct market outlets for Huehuetenango coffee to ensure growers received a fair return was a crucial objective, but it only began to be achieved in 2008 with the setting up of the *Comercializadora Baluarte Huehuetenango*. Run by the producers themselves, as of the 2009 harvest, this new body will oversee the direct sale of coffee to roasters.

'We are small producers, but hope that this project will become large,' says Manrique Lopez Castillo, coordinator of the Huehuetenango Highlands Coffee Presidium and manager of the Comercializadora. 'We are striving to shorten the supply chain by creating direct contacts between producers and roasters. We hope that our efforts will be successful and stimulate similar initiatives in other cooperatives. The Huehuetenango experience shows that improving the quality of coffee and commercializing it without intermediaries significantly improves the quality of life of producer communities.'

SET UP IN 2002, THE PROJECT HAS ALREADY ACHIEVED A GREAT DEAL. IT NOW INVOLVES 160 SMALL PRODUCERS, WHO CULTIVATE COFFEE AT ALTITUDES OF OVER 1,500 METERS.

THE CHILDREN SOW SEEDS, PLANT, CULTIVATE AND ENTHUSIASTICALLY LOOK AFTER THE GARDENS OF VEGETABLES, HERBS, BERRY BUSHES AND HEDGES.

CHILDREN IN STYRIAN SCHOOLS ARE SOWING SEEDS, CULTIVATING AND THEN EATING LOCAL PRODUCTS. AN EXAMPLE OF TASTE EDUCATION FOR CHILDREN.

Ketchup Isn't A Vegetable

Manfred Flieser
Austria, Slow Food International Councillor
and Styria Convivium leader

EDUCATION I had the idea of creating projects to raise children's awareness in the spring of 2001, two years before the Slow Food international board resolved to extend the US school gardens project during the International Naples Congress.

My project involved kids and their parents coming to a workshop where they prepared

© M. FLIESER

IN SPRING 2005 WE CUT THE RIBBON OF THE FIRST OF THE EIGHT SLOW FOOD SCHOOL GARDENS IN STYRIA. THERE ARE NOW 13 GARDENS AND EXCELLENT DEVELOPMENT PROSPECTS.

Osterbrot, a traditional sweet bread made at Easter. During the course the adults eagerly watched the master baker, following the movements of his fingers. The children enthusiastically kneaded the dough, made bread rolls and shaped the plaits for the Easter bread. Since then Slow Food Styria has organized a cookery workshop for children twice a year. It is filmed by regional television and broadcast in the early evening. 'Spaghetti and pizza' is the spontaneous reply when a TV journalist asks the children what their favorite food is. This is hardly surprising: pasta only takes six minutes to prepare and readymade sauces can be heated up in a moment. Frozen pizza which is 'ready for the oven' can be brought to the table just as quickly: 'Kids, wash your hands, the food's ready!'

Aware consumption begins with buying. Before we start cooking at a Slow Food workshop, we pick fresh, ripe produce in the garden and buy anything else at the farm. In this way city children learn the milk doesn't come from a cardboard carton and that ketchup isn't a vegetable. Farmers who keep their animals in a natural environment open the shed doors and explain how butter is made and how to press pumpkin seed oil, a Styrian specialty.

The children begin to 'understand' food and see how fresh ingredients can be used to prepare a tasty meal. Their passion for tasty and healthy food develops: even small children want to eat well and consume local seasonal produce.

THE GREEN CLASSROOM

In 2004 I managed to persuade the mayors of fifteen local authorities to set up gardens in their nursery, elementary and junior high schools. Then it was necessary to talk to school

principals and teachers. As we were all in agreement and there was funding from local and provincial authorities and the European Union (through the Leader+ initiative), we asked for authorization from the provincial education authority. It was granted without any problems. At this point we needed assistance from an expert to put our ideas into practice and see if it was possible to use the school playground or areas nearby. We were very fortunate that Theresia Krammer, the recently retired director of an agricultural institute, was able to help us in this important work.

In just three months we managed to identify areas for future gardens in five elementary schools and three nursery schools, and also to begin some planting and construction work. In choosing seeds and plants, I advised considering varieties of traditional local vegetables, fruit and berries which were tasty but had become relatively rare.

In spring 2005 we cut the ribbon of the first of the eight Slow Food school gardens in Styria. There are now 13 gardens and excellent prospects for further rapid development!

The children sow seeds, plant, cultivate and enthusiastically look after the gardens of vegetables, herbs, berry bushes and hedges. They keep a careful note of their observations, from sowing to harvesting. The fruits of their labor are not only made into tasty school snacks but are also sold as seed to the public. This makes the children very proud!

In the elementary school of Hönigtal near Graz, 23 schoolchildren grew a range of potato varieties—Cyclame, Pinki, Goldsegen, Barbara, Hermes, Viola, Rotaugerl, Unendlich Lange, Kipfler—with different shapes, colors, sizes and tastes. With the help of chef Heinz Auer the children then prepared tasty delicacies: potato goulash, traditional *Erdäpfelsterz* potato cakes, potato ravioli filled with cabbage, purple potato purée with fried eggs and a potato salad. Teachers and parents were amazed at the range of different tastes.

ARTIFICIAL FLAVORINGS AND TASTE ENHANCERS TRICK OUR EYES, NOSE AND PALATE WITH SOMETHING THAT ISN'T THERE.

TRAINING THE SENSES

With the progressive spread of ready-made meals, Styrian families are also cooking less frequently. The reflection that artificial flavorings and taste enhancers trick our eyes, nose and palate with something that isn't there prompted a decision to create sensory education initiatives. Slow Food Styria has developed the *Essen & Trinken mit allen Sinnen wahrnehmen*, (Eat and Drink with all the Senses) program. This project was first introduced to nursery and elementary schools in the Hügelland, a hilly district east of Graz, with the sensory education initiative complementing the Slow Food school gardens project.

To show how much our eyes are influenced by colors or how our imagination causes us to perceive a particular taste, I recently asked a group of students at the Fachhochschule Joanneum in Bad Gleichenberg to taste some apple juice. It was natural juice to which I had added tasteless green, red or orange food coloring. Even the oldest students were tricked by the colors: none of them realized that the juice was always the same!

After evaluating hundreds of questionnaires about what students ate for breakfast and snacks, the board of the Hügelland decided to organize a cooking workshop and asked Slow Food Styria to prepare a project and compile a cookbook. Since spring 2008 all the students of the region have received a copy of the *Slow Food Styria Frühstück & Jausen-Kochbuch* cookbook.

Children and students are very interested in our projects and pass on what they learn to their parents and siblings. We are confident that the aims of the project will be achieved. Children have been stimulated to choose seasonal food produced by local farmers and artisans, and are enthusiastic about food that is very different from ready-made meals and fast food. As is well known, enthusiastic children can move mountains and they are the ones to improve the consumption and eating behavior of their parents.

The *White* Supertuscan

THE ARDA VALLEY

Dessislava Dimitrova
Bulgaria, a biologist specialized in botany

LOCAL ECONOMY

I must admit that I am not an economist and the invitation to write an article on local economy was a great challenge for me. But then I remembered that local economy also means the efforts of people to live well and in harmony with their environment, traditions and culture. Economists who expect profound specialized analysis on this topic will be disappointed. This is an article for people who love small things, who enjoy good food, who want to meet the producer of this food and who may even participate in the process of food production. This is an article inspired by smells and tastes from the past and is targeted at people who seek them in the present and try to preserve them for the future. Nowadays, in a world in which planes fly us to the most remote places in the world and communications shorten the distance between us to a few seconds, we human beings have almost forgotten such simple pleasures as preparing dinner for the family, drinking a glass of home-made wine with a neighbor, picking vegetables and fruit from the garden and starting the new day with the song of the nightingale or the morning sounds of a wakening village. These are my memories of my childhood. Today, my daughter can enjoy all this only when we go on vacation to the countryside.

ARE YOU HAPPY?

Competing against time, people from the big cities are completely unaware of the livelihood of small communities in the countryside. The inhabitants of a small village hardly believe that their food, their lifestyle, their hospitality and their warmth might be sought after by exhausted and emotionally worn-out people from the big cities. This is how the two parts of one thing (the human being) meet and this is a powerful stimulus for the development of local economies. The diversity of local economies—small-scale food production, green tourism, eco-tourism, rural tourism, farmers' markets—is as colorful and lively as the countryside itself. Here are some of the many ways in which the need for good, clean and fair lifestyle is satisfied.

IN THEIR QUEST FOR A MORE PLEASANT AND EXCITING LIFE, PEOPLE VERY OFTEN BEGIN BY REVIVING LOCAL TRADITIONS, INCLUDING FOOD CULTURE, THAT CAN GROW INTO SMALL-SCALE ECONOMIC ENTERPRISES. OPPOSITE, SMILYAN BEANS.

PROTECTING
NATURE

In my opinion, there are two major ways through which people discover the local economy as a potential for a healthier, more pleasant life. People in economically developed countries have experienced the strong destructive potential of industrialization both in everyday life and in nature. Some time ago I read about a modern methodology to measure happiness! Where is mankind heading for, if it needs a scientific approach to measure the most natural feeling of a human being? In their quest for a more pleasant and exciting life, people very often begin by reviving local traditions (including food culture) that can grow into small-scale economic enterprises. People are trying to find ways to shorten the distance between producers and consumers, to make the connections between them more direct and to make these economic activities a benefit for the local community. This leads to the preservation of the livelihoods of local farm families, hotel keepers and other members of the community. At the same time, the impact of consumers over the kind and quality of their food becomes stronger and makes them responsible actors in the preservation of local traditions, nature and the landscapes. Hence everybody in the local community has a direct, long-term interest in the prosperity, health, and beauty of their homeland.

NATURAL TREASURES

In countries facing economic difficulties, the small-scale economy is an efficient way to overcome low production rates, land abandonment, depopulation, destruction of habitats and landscapes and loss of wild and domestic species diversity. The small success of

a single family leads to the natural need for cooperation among the members of the community, which gradually gains in strength. The local community thus achieves the power to resist aggressive construction companies, mass-tourism operators and so on, who would otherwise deprive them of their identity.

I still have to figure out the characteristics of a community that can develop into a lively local economic entity. But I can tell you the story of a picturesque valley inhabited by inventive people who want to preserve their treasures of culture, nature and tradition and serve them as a precious gift to their guests. Somewhere near the Greek border, in the Central Rhodopi Mountains in Bulgaria, is the source of the Arda river. The upper part of the valley is a patchwork of small dwellings perched on hills, meandering streams, old forests, mountain meadows and pastures, parcels of land cultivated with beans and potatoes and, above all, a fascinating mixture of traditions, handicrafts and tastes that have been preserved by the locals for centuries. The Upper Arda river valley is inhabited by more than 5,000 people, among whom the

THE LOCAL COMMUNITY HAS REALIZED THAT THEY HAVE AN UNDISCOVERED TREASURE IN THEIR HANDS:
HIGH-VALUE NATURAL RESOURCES AND A STILL VIVID TRADITIONAL LIVELIHOOD.

SUSTAINABLE COMMUNITY
DEVELOPMENT

percentage of young and active people is relatively high compared to other mountain areas in Bulgaria. People in the area are not interested in mass tourism because it is very close to them already (the Pamporovo ski resort is only 20 km away) and they have seen the negative effects it can have on nature and lifestyle. The local community has realized that they have an undiscovered treasure in their hands: high-value natural resources and a still vivid traditional livelihood.

TALK TO SAFADIN

Life is not easy for the local people in the villages along the Upper Arda river. When a visitor walks around here, he or she might think that the people have lost their hope, their will to change and their self-confidence. Then suddenly they see a small and attractive hotel or a guesthouse, there to prove that the spring of energy and will has not dried up and that people want to improve their lives to provide young people with an alternative to migration to the cities. Now that access to the area is freer, different forms of soft tourism are considered as major sources of income and potential for future development and motivation, especially for young people keen to return and work for the wellbeing of their birthplace. The guesthouses and small family hotels that have appeared in the last decade offer comfortable accommodation and delicious Rhodopi cuisine.

When I first visited the place four years ago to identify communities for participation at the first Terra Madre event, I was surprised to find how close the Slow Food philosophy is to the local people. My first meetings with

them showed they had already discovered the uniqueness of their Smilyan beans and had organized activities related to them. One such is the Festival of Smilyan Beans, held on the last Saturday of November since 2003. Participation at Terra Madre 2004 and 2006 provided a strong impetus for the local community to search for 'forgotten' foods and revive food culture and traditions, thus identifying the scope and goals of a local Slow Food-oriented community of producers. One understands better the perceptions of the local community when one talks with Safidin, the mayor of one of the villages, Veneta and Milkana, co-founders of a small dairy, and Banko, the owner of one of the hotels in the village. They are some of the members of the Rhodopi-Smilyan Convivium, and each of them conveys, in a different way, his or her ties with the land, for them a precious commodity. They and others like them constitute a sort of driving force that could set off a broader process, fueled by the will to change the Bulgarian perception of 'development', promoting sustainable development based on local resources and traditions.

SERRALUNGA D'ALBA. THE FONTANAFREDDA BAROLO
Barolo
Denominazione di Origine Controllata e Garantita
Serralunga d'Alba
FONTANAFREDDA
2004
A UNIQUE TERROIR THAT PRODUCES A PARTICULARLY HIGHLY-PRIZED BAROLO, WITH GREAT STRUCTURE AND A STRONG PERSONALITY: THE BAROLO OF SERRALUNGA D'ALBA.
WWW.FONTANAFREDDA.IT

THE ALTERNATIVE

Gianluca Brunori,
Italy, professor of agrarian economics at the University of Pisa

LOCAL ECONOMY

Globalization has changed the organization of things and people in space and time radically. It has taken 'space-time compression', the true motor of the development of capitalism, to its extreme consequences, creating enormous infrastructures capable of making resources circulate from one part of the planet to another in a ridiculously short space of time.

According to the sociologist Manuel Castells, these processes have led to the distinction between a space of places and a space of flows. The first is a continuous space, contained within well-defined boundaries, shaped by material and immaterial elements that accumulate in time and which reveal internal coherence and a clear differentiation from the outside. The second is a discontinuous space, made of spatially localized nodes connected by flows of things, people and information; it is continuously transformed by the restructuring of the constructed environment necessary to govern the flow of goods.

The space of places is governed by history and culture, while the space of flows is governed by technology and the market.

TWO-FACED JANUS

The American farmer-intellectual Wendell Berry contrasts local economies, which develop in the space of places, with total economies, which characterize the space of flows. Local economies are based on the local control of economic activities and economic behavior is closely interwoven with and influenced by the place's characteristic norms and values. In total economies everything has a price and can be bought and sold, and the most important decisions are made by corporations and global institutions.

Faced with the expansion of the total economy, local economies are forced to withdraw. Deprived of the necessary economic base, the spaces of places lose the ability to reproduce their difference and gradually melt into the space of flows, which empties or fills them according to global market conditions. Among the most conspicuous

SYMBOLIC, RELATIONAL
PHYSICAL RELOCATION

examples of the relationship between total and local economies is the unregulated opening of large supermarkets in a local areas. When this happens, people often react favorably insofar as supermarkets promise a large variety of cheap commodities. But the closure of small commercial enterprises, no longer capable of standing up to the competition, creates unemployment, turns towns into deserts, increases car-dependence among consumers, excludes people without their own means of transport and non-drivers and eliminating commercial opportunities for local products, thus jeopardizing their survival.

The unopposed domination of the total economy does not generate greater well-being. The wealth created is the other face of the destruction wrought; the transition stages generate intolerable suffering; inequalities and concentrations of power grow. The destruction of local economies and the subsequent withdrawal of the space of places is at the root of the loss of economic, cultural and biological diversity, which represent the basic conditions for the survival of the delicate balance between humankind and nature. The creation of a counterpoise to the total economy through the strengthening of local economies is a commitment that ought to concern anyone who cares about the fate of humanity. A relocation process reinforcing local control over economic processes and promoting local resources is thus highly desirable.

CONSCIOUS CONSUMPTION

At the moment, relocation processes are primarily fueled by grass-roots movements, which in just a few years have grown significantly, generating growing awareness in civil society, in the economic fabric and in institutions. Through these groups' initiative, relocation has taken on a symbolic, relational and physical dimension. Symbolic relocation means reinforcing awareness of the value of local resources—biodiversity, the landscape, culture, social networks—and of the origin of goods to enable economic actors to take informed and responsible decisions. If consumers know where the good they are consuming is from, they can grow aware of the exploitation of the environment and people that has allowed it to be produced and distributed. If local producers are in a position to communicate to consumers the value that the use of local resources adds to the final product, they can create a situation that is advantageous for both.

Relational relocation means encouraging relationships of exchange among local actors. Studies in the United Kingdom have shown that, spending on shopping being equal, purchases in local shops keep 40 percent of income within the community.

The time banks that are spreading everywhere draw leverage from the ability of the members of a community to supply goods or services that the market or institutions

SYMBOLIC RELOCATION MEANS REINFORCING AWARENESS OF THE VALUE OF LOCAL RESOURCES AND OF THE ORIGIN OF GOODS TO ENABLE ECONOMIC ACTORS TO TAKE INFORMED AND RESPONSIBLE DECISIONS.

TO TAKE ACTION ON THE SIGNIFICANCES OF FOOD IS TO TAKE ACTION ON EVERYDAY PRACTICES: SMALL CHANGES
IN INDIVIDUAL CHOICES MAY LEAD TO MAJOR COLLECTIVE CHANGES.

CONSUMERS AND PRODUCERS

are unable to provide. Solidarity purchasing groups establish a channel of communication between consumers and producers based on common values that forms of awareness and a consumption ethic external to commercial relations.

Physical relocation, finally, involves the restructuring of production, distribution

erence for local produce, fresh with a low environmental impact, or in the choice of typical produce, testaments of the identity of other places. When consumers choose a local food product that incorporates and promotes local resources, they do their bit in maintaining those resources and supporting strengthening local

MEANINGS OF FOOD

and consumption to favor, when possible, the cutting of distances and commercial brokerage.

CHOICES AND RESOURCES

Food is a fundamental starting point for relocation movements. It symbolizes relations between humans, society and nature. It is an essential good, but at the same time satisfies deep needs for identification and sociality; above all, it concerns everyone, no one excluded. To take action on the significances of food is to take action on everyday practices, and small changes in individual choices, repeated day by day, may lead to major collective changes.

Symbolic and relational relocation permit physical relocation, materializing in pref-

producers against the total economy. Farmers' markets, Community Supported Agriculture initiatives, the introduction of local and organic products to schools, solidarity purchasing groups, fair trade, Slow Food presidia and 'food miles' awareness campaigns are driving forces for symbolic, relational and physical relocation. They are now moving beyond the embryonic phase to become a broad, widespread movement. The building of solid local economies depends on the ability of such movements to transform personal lifestyles to the quick, to encourage extension to other areas of consumption, to grant continuity to alternative productive models and to allow the conditions for the updating of public regulations to mature.

LEBANON'S SLOW FOOD MARKETS ARE A UNIQUE OCCASION NOT ONLY FOR

SELLING AND BUYING FOOD BUT ALSO TO FIND OUT MORE ABOUT THE COUNTRY'S

GASTRONOMIC IDENTITY.

SOUK EVERY MONDAY

Rami Zurayk

Lebanon, professor of Ecosystem Management at the American University
of Beirut and a founder of the Slow Food Beirut Convivium

LOCAL ECONOMY

The past decade has seen an exponential increase in the number of farmers' markets in the world. In the US alone, their number increased from 1,755 in 1994 to 3,700 in 2004, and they served more than 3 million consumers. They have been hailed and praised as essential components of local food systems. They provide an alternative to supermarkets and large food corporations, which are the pillars of the globalized food system that dominates our lives. They are especially appropriate for entrepreneurial small farmers seeking to establish short supply chains (and therefore increase their profit margins) by personal selling of high quality products. It is estimated that direct selling will result in the producer receiving 80-90 percent of the food dollar instead of the usual 8-10 percent in conventional market channels.

Farmers' markets sit at the convergence of a number of disciplines: civic engagement, public health, environment, sustainable agriculture, transportation, historic preservation, and local economy. They benefit communities by providing economic opportunities and sustainable livelihoods, promoting healthy eating and public health, creating active public space, shaping growth, revitalizing downtowns and neighborhoods and by bringing diverse people together. The linkages they provide between producers and consumers go beyond business operations to encompass social relationships.

NABATIYYEH

Lebanon is mostly known for the protracted wars that have plagued it since 1975. Few people realize that Lebanon's other problems also include a political system based on sectarianism (religious identity) and an economic regime anchored in market fundamentalism. Sectarianism has resulted in the creation of divisions and mistrust between the different sects, while ultra-liberalism has contributed to the deepening of

poverty
and the breakdown of local food
production systems.

Long before the emergence of the current
retail agribusiness systems, farmers' markets (or producers' markets) were the basis
of community food distribution systems in
Lebanon. Local markets (souks) are still
held in most rural towns of the country, especially in the south. These weekly markets
take place on a specific day and offer an opportunity for purchasing goods from itiner-
ant vendors.

The most famous souk in south Lebanon
is the Nabatiyyeh, traditionally held every
Monday. Historical records dating back to

the 19th century indicate that the Nabatiyyeh souk attracted people from the four corners of the region. Writing in 1860, the chronicler Chaker el Khoury reports 5,000 to 6,000 individuals attending every week and of over 50,000 transactions taking place during one day. He also describes it as a meeting place for people of all creeds: Christians, Muslims, Druze and Jews. Today, the Nabatiyyeh market is still vibrant but, as in the other town markets in Lebanon, many of the goods on offer are imported from as far away as China. Moreover, the diversity that used to characterize it once has been much reduced by war, polarization and division in Lebanese society.

SOUK EL ARD

It is against a background of conflict, internal strife and social inequality that the project entitled 'Support to Local Agricultural Markets as a Means to Promote the Development of Agricultural Production in Lebanon' was created. The project is funded by the ROSS Program, an Italian Ministry of Foreign Affairs initiative to help in the reconstruction of Lebanon after the Israeli bombings of July 2006. It is implemented by an Italian NGO, UCODEP, in partnership with Slow Food Beirut and the Slow Food Foundation for Biodiversity.

The main objective of the project is to help small Lebanese farmers gain access to the local market by opening three weekly farmers' markets. These are located in the coastal cities of Tripoli, Beirut and Saida. The markets, named 'Souk el Ard' (Earth Markets), are part of the international Earth Markets network created by Slow Food. They share Slow Food's commitment to good, clean and fair products and to the revival of local food systems. They also offer a means of revitalizing local production of regional specialties and seasonal traditions.

In 2007-2008, two out of the three planned markets were inaugurated. The Tripoli market opened on December 6. It is located in one of the most beautiful parts of the city, the capital of North Lebanon. The market takes place every Thursday in a public garden made available by the municipality of Al Mina ('The Port'), right next to the esplanade bordering the fishing harbor. There are about 20 stalls, all occupied by small producers. There are organic vegetable growers, processed food manufacturers and a few stalls selling hand-made natural products and

of their very local nature. This view is especially common among staunch believers in the global capitalist economy, who exhort export-oriented production and use low cost per unit of product as a measure of market efficiency. This approach overlooks the 'ecological footprint' of food production (environmental costs of production and transport), the food quality loss as a result of long distance trade as well as the physical

EARTH
MARKETS

pottery cooking utensils. The market is managed by Souk el Tayeb, a private enterprise with experience in market management which founded the Souk el Tayeb producers' market in Beirut in 2004.

Saida is the capital of South Lebanon, and, like Tripoli, is a historic city with the remains of Phoenician temples and crusaders' castles. The Saida farmers' market opened its doors on April 7 2007. It is located in Khan el Franj, the old caravanserai in the old city, right next door to the old vaulted souk of Saida. This is where the caravans carrying spices and brocades from the Incense Road and the Silk Road used to park, in the safety of the great wooden gates. Saida's Souk el Ard takes place every Sunday. It is managed by Slow Food Beirut, in collaboration with the producers themselves and with the Hariri Foundation, a Lebanese NGO. A board of trustees composed of social entrepreneurs from the city of Saida will be formed to offer guidance to the market and to promote it among the local community.

ECOLOGICAL IMPACT

Research on the economic efficiency of farmers' markets is still rare. Many analysts believe that their impact is small because

waste associated with wholesale markets. It also ignores the social costs of large-scale farming usually associated with the loss of livelihoods of small producers due to farm consolidation necessary to support an extended wholesale system. Moreover, by helping small farmers and organic producers stay in business, markets directly contribute to the preservation of open space and the maintenance of the rural landscape. Today, this is an imperative need in Lebanon as in any other country.

However, Souk el Ard provide an extra set of benefits very specific to Lebanon. They function as meeting places for people from all walks of life, producers and customers, who might never have interacted otherwise. In Lebanon, where internal strife is always looming, the existence of a 'neutral' environment where people from all confessions and all regions freely intermingle is a necessity for the survival of society. Bringing together Lebanese (and foreigners) from all social classes and from the four corners of the country is an invaluable service to society. In Souk el Ard one finds Good, Clean, Fair as well as Peace products. This may well be the markets' most precious contribution of all.

LONG BEFORE THE EMERGENCE OF THE CURRENT RETAIL AGRIBUSINESS SYSTEMS, FARMERS' MARKETS WERE THE BASIS OF COMMUNITY FOOD DISTRIBUTION SYSTEMS.

THE YALE GENERATION

Joshua Viertel
USA, director of the Yale Sustainable Food Project

LOCAL ECONOMY

Yale alumni have run in every US Presidential election since 1972. The university produces an astounding number of leaders—in politics, in business, in social movements and in communities. The Yale Sustainable Food Project works to create a new generation of leaders who understand and appreciate the deep connections among people, land and food, and who value ecology, culture and taste more than power or money.

The Project was founded in 2001 in the belief that the world's most pressing questions regarding health, culture, the environment, education, and the global economy can only be adequately addressed if we consider the food we eat and the way we produce it. We aim to foster a culture that draws meaning and pleasure from the connections among people, land and food, so that students will go into the world knowing how to nourish themselves, their communities and the land. We do this by making food and agriculture an integral part of education and everyday life at Yale: we collaborate with faculty and students to increase academic work related to food and agriculture on campus, we run diverse extra-curricular educational programs, we manage an organic farm on campus, and we direct a sustainable dining program in Yale's dining halls.

FRESHERS ON THE FARM

A university is designed to educate, and we believe that knowledge about food and agriculture is an integral part of the liberal education offered at Yale. To that end, we collaborate with professors to increase course offerings in a range of departments; in the 2007-2008 academic year, there were 26 courses related to food and agriculture offered to Yale undergraduates. The co-directors of the Project have acted as guest lecturers in many of these courses; they also teach a yearly seminar in sustainable food and agriculture. We try to seed every department with courses on food and agriculture, but we have also created a cohesive course of study in food in agriculture by collaborating with the Program in Environmental Studies. We hope that this program—

which allows students to concentrate their four years of study in food and agriculture—will prepare future environmental leaders to approach problems with a deep awareness of the ways that agriculture and food affect our landscape, our ecology, our culture and our lives.

We also ensure that extra-curricular education on food and agriculture is part of Yale's landscape, through the Harvest pre-orientation program and through an annual series of

able agriculture and about the pleasure of sharing good work and good food. The wood-fired oven at the Yale Farm—built in 2005 by Yale students with guidance from a father-son team of masons—is at the heart of what we do. Each Friday, we mark the end of the harvest by preparing a meal from the farm's produce, and sharing it with volunteers.

The Farm is a four-season market garden; during the academic year, student farm man-

FRESHERS ON FARMS

speakers, workshops, and films on campus. On Harvest, groups of freshmen spend the week before they begin school on a family-owned farm in Connecticut. Led by upper-classmen, these freshmen learn about food production and the local landscape while making some of their first friends at Yale. Each year, we bring in a range of speakers—authors like Michael Pollan and Eric Schlosser, chefs/activists like Odessa Piper, Ann Cooper and Alice Waters, and food scientist Hal McGee, among others—to address issues of food, agriculture and sustainability. We teach workshops on topics from baking bread in a wood-fired oven to winter gardening, believing that a practical education is a necessary supplement to an academic one. Students gain concrete skills through these workshops, but more importantly they are seduced both by the pleasure that comes from engaging in the process that creates their food and by sharing meaningful work with their peers.

GARDENS & CAFETERIAS

The Yale Farm is the place where this process and this engagement are most tangible. On our farm, we seek to model sustainable agricultural practices and educate both Yale students and the community about sustain-

agers run the farm through three weekly volunteer workdays. In the summer, we offer an internship through which six Yale undergraduates spend the summer working full-time on the farm. Graduates of the internship have gone on to create their own farms, build educational programs on urban agriculture and work in the non-profit sector on food and agriculture issues.

The Farm also allows Yale students to engage with the wider New Haven community; we sell most of our produce at a local farmers' market in New Haven. The students who sell our produce meet and learn from local farmers and interact with local residents who shop there, becoming an integral part of the local economy and community.

In addition to our academic work and programming at the farm, the Sustainable Food Project collaborates with Yale's Dining Services to increase the amount of sustainable food being served in Yale's dining halls. Schools teach lasting lessons about ethics through their everyday practices, and we help Yale to model practices that are sustainable, just and delicious, hoping that the values those practices represent will make their way into our students' lives. What began as a pilot program in just one of Yale's dining halls has now expanded to reach every

ON THE CAMPUS FARM WE SEEK TO MODEL SUSTAINABLE AGRICULTURAL PRACTICES AND EDUCATE STUDENTS AND COMMUNITY ABOUT SUSTAINABLE AGRICULTURE AND PLEASURE.

FOOD AND
SUSTAINABLE AGRICULTURE

dining hall on campus. This has meant changing menus so that they reflect what's available in the region rather than arbitrary cycles of food items, training cooks in new food preparation techniques, developing distribution networks composed of local farmers and processors, and developing recipes that reflect our region but also engage with a range of food traditions to reflect the diversity of Yale College as a whole. In the 2006-2007 academic year, Yale spent $1.6 million in the local economy by buying food from local farmers and processing it locally.

CARBON & FOOD

When the sustainable food project was founded in 2001, it was an uncharted territory. Today, students at universities across the US are turning their attention to food systems in efforts to address campus sustainability and social responsibility. In the fall of 2007, Yale hosted a summit attended by 150 student delegates from schools in the northeastern United States, each of whom was a leader in the sustainable food movement on his or her campus. Some of the delegates at that summit were selected as student delegates for Slow Food's International Congress in Puebla. The presentation they made there, in partnership with the international students from the University of Gastronomic Sciences, was instrumental in building momentum to bring youth into Slow Food's focus and to bring youth to Terra Madre. Universities are beginning to understand the need to be environmentally responsible, and beginning to measure themselves according to their carbon footprint. This is a good start, but the ecological footprint of a university's operations is quickly dwarfed by the leaders that university produces and the decisions they make. We do significantly reduce Yale's carbon footprint through changing the way Yale eats. But we hope that change will pale in comparison to the changes made by the young people who graduate from Yale with a real understanding of the food they eat and the way it is produced. Our hope is that one day Yale will produce a graduate who has worked on a local organic farm as part of her fresher orientation, who has eaten local, grass-fed beef in Yale's dining halls, and who has written a senior thesis on the connections between food, culture and politics, graduating with honors with a major in sustainable food and agriculture. We hope that she will take all that she learned in her time at Yale and she will use it well when, like so many Yale graduates before her, she is elected to be the president of the United States.

UNIVERSITIES ARE BEGINNING TO UNDERSTAND THE NEED TO BE ENVIRONMENTALLY RESPONSIBLE, AND BEGINNING TO MEASURE THEMSELVES ACCORDING TO THEIR CARBON FOOTPRINT.

CUES FOR CHANGE IN COLLECTIVE AND HOSPITAL CATERING. THE SLOW FOOD MOVEMENT AND NEW SCENARIOS.

The Taste for Health

Andrea Pezzana
Italy, a physician and director of the SSCVD Dietetics and Nutrition
Clinic at the San Giovanni Antica Sede hospital in Turin

EDUCATION

Carlo Petrini has explained and clarified the continuous evolution of Slow Food's philosophy and activities in *Slow Food Nation* (Rizzoli, 2007). One of the many stimulating points in the book is the redefinition of the 'consumer' as a 'co-producer', as an individual closely involved in the food production and commercializa-

tion chains with objective possibilities of driving the market through the choice to buy or not to buy what the market itself makes available on a daily basis. The major novelty is the introduction of criteria of responsibility, competence and awareness among the minimum requirements of our daily food choices.

Moving on to a question deeply rooted in daily life, we immediately think about where and when 'everyday' food is consumed. For most workers and students, this means canteens, dining halls, self-service restaurants, cafeterias: in other words, large-scale collective catering services.

Today these services are the most important for consumers, or co-producers, buying, preparing and serving millions of meals every day, influencing the market considerably and orienting it towards 'virtuous' (seasonal, short supply chain, quality) foods or to foods sourced according to random or solely economic criteria.

In recent years, Slow Food Italy has promoted an increasing number of initiatives with institutional and private partners to increase knowledge and awareness of everyday eating behavior. They have included collaborations with university cafeterias in Piedmont (for example, EDISU in Turin and UNISG in Pollenzo), the realization of the Italian 'School Garden Project' and the organization of conferences and events.

Particularly worthy of mention is the partnership of the Italian Ministry of Health and other associations on the 'Gaining Health - Making healthy choices easy' program, promoted in the squares of Rome, Turin, Milan and Naples in June 2007. The initiative was designed to attract people to the concept of a healthy lifestyle, promote quality food products and stimulate the sensorial recognition of excellent products.

THERAPIES IN A BITE

Slow Food's adventure in the world of hospital food service began in October 2004 with the signing of the Protocol Agreement between Slow Food Italy, the Piedmont Regional Authority and the San Giovanni Battista Hospital in Turin.

The signing of this document set off a series of initiatives for the patients and the staff (as well as their families) of the San Giovanni Hospital. The purpose was to bring to the hospital environment some of the themes that had already inspired other Slow Food projects: regaining the appeal of food, a sense of home and conviviality and its profound influence on well-being. In recognition of the fact that food in the health field has a therapeutic value, the intent was to amplify the value and potential of food during treatment and recovery.

The document that inspired the project was the *Charter of the patient's right to pleasure, conviviality and food quality*. The charter is divided into four parts that reassert the primary value of food in the health care field, its therapeutic and convivial aspects, its role in health education and promotion and its value as an indicator of the quality of treatment.

Though it has yet to exert a strong impact on the daily nutrition of patients and staff, the big innovation of taste-sensory workshops in a cancer ward deserve to be mentioned. The tried and tested Master of Food educational model has been amplified and supplemented with observations and dietetic-nutritional interventions designed to protect and recover the health of patients through daily eating. Even 'holiday' food has been a subject for taste workshops, which have helped the participants to recover not only their sense of taste, but also symbolic values, pleasure and cultural and nutritional meaning.

Between December 2004 and December 2007, there were about 30 'Taste for Health' workshops dedicated to various themes, including: chocolate, cheese, rice, holiday desserts, peppers, mint tea, *La Granda* Presidium beef, fish, *bagna caoda* (a local Piedmontese dip of oil, garlic and salted anchovies accompanied by winter vegetables), pesto and basil, ice-cream, cooking with flowers, daily groceries, packaging and reading labels. The workshops were intro-

SLOW FOOD'S ADVENTURE IN THE WORLD OF HOSPITAL FOOD SERVICE BEGAN IN OCTOBER 2004. THE DOCUMENT INSPIRING THE ENTIRE PROJECT IS THE CHARTER OF THE PATIENT'S RIGHT TO PLEASURE, CONVIVIALITY AND FOOD QUALITY.

duced by assessments of the wholesomeness of foodstuffs and suggested 'user instructions' in the event of health and illness, with specific references to possible side-effects, especially for patients undergoing cancer treatment (chemotherapy and radiotherapy).

The experience has aroused so much interest that it has been referred to in papers and speeches at scientific congresses on the subject of nutrition.

Despite early reluctance, in the course of time the number of enquiries and requests for collaboration—first from individuals, then from Italian and foreign hospitals — has increased.

SEASONS IN THE WARD

During the Salone del Gusto 2006, a round table was organized to discuss 'Recovery Comes with Eating: good, clean and fair in hospital food service'. Thanks to the presence of the Health Minister, Livia Turco, Piedmont's Regional Councilor for Health Protection, Mario Valpreda, the President of the Italian Association of Dietetics and Clinical Nutrition (ADI), Maria Antonia Fusco, and with the friendly guidance of host Carlo Petrini, the discussion helped shape a scenario that had previously been inconceivable.

The event marked the beginning of communication and, subsequently, lively collaboration amongst politicians, local administrators, gastronomes, nutritionists, dieticians and health administrators, treasurers, managers and so on—in other words, all the subjects involved, at various levels, in the planning, management and assessment of hospital food services. Between March and July 2007, a technical commission of representatives of Slow Food Italy, the ADI and the Ministry of Health prepared an operational path in various stages. An evaluation of existing hospital food services will be followed by practical suggestions to allow the most attentive and innovative facilities to review the organization and management of hospital meals from a nutritional, gastronomic and eco-environmental perspective.

In this sense, the recommendations of the European Council, promulgated in 2003, have been a constant point of reference and a stated objective.

The final outcome will see patients and hospital workers enjoying better meals characterized by seasonality, freshness and respect for the environment.

While it is as yet impossible to speak in terms of a codified model, the ongoing study should help open up new potential for local markets often excluded from a collective food service that is part of the large-scale national distribution framework.

Though the road ahead is still a long one, examples such as the Alice Foundation in Darmstadt in Germany and the new Asti Hospital in Italy have already demonstrated the feasibility of the project. Bureaucratic delays and organizational requirements do not help small producers to become part of the logic of collective food services. It is thus important for small local economies to review their organization and logistics if they are to become more incisive and widespread on such markets.

CARDINAL MASSAIA

Since January 2008, Cardinal Massaia Hospital, run by the Asti local health authority, has based the preparation of the 1,700 dishes made each day for the patients and staff on local tradition. The choice focuses on quality produce from Asti and Piedmont, cooked simply and heightened with fresh aromatic herbs. In the wards it is now possible to find classic Piedmontese *agnolotti* from an artisan company in Mondovì and carnaroli and balilla rice from the province of Vercelli. Meat—beef from Val Bormida (Cuneo), raw or cooked—alternates with fish and regional cheeses, such as Bra duro, Raschera and Robiola di Roccaverano. Fruit and vegetables are seasonal and the main condiment is extra virgin olive oil from western Liguria. This new model of hospital food service is based on the therapeutic value of nutrition, particularly its emotional, cultural and convivial qualities, and stresses the importance of meals that encourage short food supply chains, traceability and seasonality.

ALICE HOSPITAL

Alice Hospital is a private clinic in Darmstadt, in the German region of Hesse. Since the autumn of 2007, local and seasonal ingredients have been used in its kitchens in the preparation of meals for patients and staff, as well as for diners in the restaurant inside the health facility. The choice was inspired by the slow philosophy and implemented thanks to the energy and initiative of the cook at Alice Hospital, Dagmar Vogel, Terra Madre delegate and member of Slow Food.

The 'Genesen-Genießen' (recover-taste) project has created a local food network that satisfies all its members. The small producers in the region—selected according to precise criteria and guidelines developed by Fabien Jauss, former student at the UNISG—are proud to take part in this social project. Moreover, they have the advantage of being able to plan their activities with greater certainty, since Dagmar Vogel agrees in advance with the farmers about what he wants to put on the table the next year so they can cultivate the necessary crops.

The kitchen staff performs gratifying work, creating new recipes with seasonal foods aimed at helping patients recover.

So what about the patients? Their more than positive opinion about the quality of the meals has helped to spread the clinic's fame and to publicize a clearer picture of the philosophy and activities of the Slow Food movement. Press and television continue to highlight 'Genesen-Genießen' by reporting the growing interest in better and healthier nutrition at the community level. It should also be pointed out that the increasing number of meals (all reasonably priced) eaten in the internal restaurant also help to finance the project.

Not that the project is without difficulties too. To satisfy the needs of a facility with 400 beds, many more small producers need be found and a delivery service created to distribute the food. Hence the need to plan the ahead, preparing material for patients so that they will continue to use the local produce even after they have been discharged, and creating a network of hospitals with the same ideals as Alice Hospital.

EPICURUS DOCET

Alberto Capatti
Italy, professor of the History of Cuisine and Gastronomy
at the University of Gastronomic Sciences, Pollenzo

PLEASURE

'The beginning and the root of all good is the pleasure of the stomach; even wisdom and culture must be referred to this.'[1] The aphorism, attributed to Epicurus in Athenaeus's compilation *The Deipnosophists* (dinner-table philosophers) near the end of the 2nd century AD, is hard to understand in the light of Christian culture. It finds a few echoes only in the gastronomic offshoots of 17th-century French philosophy. To define the pleasure of the stomach in terms of 'wisdom' is to transcend convivial refinement and the sharpened exercise of the senses; it is to subject the brain and thought to the test of the senses. To think that at the root of 'every good' are the study, tasting, appreciation and digestion of food is to pass over the first paradox and venture into an exercise of morality with no other intrinsic justifications than good cooking. No philosopher has ever been so radical and polemical.

The idea of pleasure that has circulated at Slow Food for 20 years would appear to have nothing to do with this maxim. The idea surfaced gradually, a little at a time, yielding to other needs whenever the occasion arose.

Within the ambit of the association and gastronomy, it eroded Third-World food morality, as an antidote to the doctrinal nature of approaches to wine or cheese, as a principle of freedom in front before an act—that of eating—that imposes rules and rituals. The slow integration into the sciences of gastronomy, seen as a culture explicitly formulated in the early 19th century and progressively acknowledged as an authoritative form of food knowledge up to the establishment of the University of Gastronomic Sciences, has allowed us to rediscover the thinking of writers such as Grimod de La Reynière and Brillat-Savarin, who really did believe that 'the pleasure of the stomach' was a matter of 'wisdom and culture' and that, thanks to the radical criticism of Christianity, they were justified in thinking that it was, if not 'the root of every good' then at least a very important 'good'. After the Revolution, the negation of values such as God, the monarchy and philosophy itself had led them to consider the senses as an overriding sphere of thought, the senses naturally being oriented towards a bidirectional object—namely, food and love.

THE RESPONSE OF SLOW FOOD TO THESE DOUBTS, WHICH TENDED TO MINIMIZE THE SIGNIFICANCE OF PLEASURE OR TO REDUCE ITS AUTHORITY, HAS BEEN TO CHANGE THE CONCEPT OF GASTRONOMY ITSELF.

A PRINCIPLE
OF FREEDOM

In a relativist era, the radicalization of thought is an eminently critical act that can assume aspects as liberticidal as they are utopian. That an association does not venture into this territory, keeping itself well away from political calculations and democratic strategies, but equally has as its reference point that pleasure of the stomach which no political candidate or thinker has ever adopted in their discourses, is in itself curious. A follower of Voltaire would advance the hypothesis that the pleasure of the stomach implies a sectarian morality, like phallus worship, the elevation of the host or the hunter's cult of the prey. Yet none of this—or any of the other more innocuous temptations, such as worshipping wine, venerating the earth, Mother Earth, or promoting a mystique of the senses through tastings—has ever materialized. Instead, the pleasure of the stomach as a foundation of convivial discourse has invested foodstuffs with all its critical force, not just as a resource for the future and mirror of the past, but also as the very reason for our responsibility towards other people.

The pleasure of the stomach welcomed by some as a moral principle, by others as an ineluctable experience, by still others as a mere trifle, has freed the association from fair-trade morals and subjection to altruism, reintroducing the principle of subjectivity into gastronomic culture. With this, the Slow Food member is not alienated by his or her own conception of good, arriving at the hypothesis that this conception can coincide with the conception of others, also in the act of drinking an 'imperfect' wine or returning to an osteria not to judge it according to the parameters of the Slow Food guide, but to re-experience a proven sense of well-being. From here to think that other 'goods' do not also exist is a large step, or rather caution is needed to proceed in this direction. Once a path has been chosen, in fact, one can go very far, and from simply enjoying food move on to become a taster and interpreter of the best food, imagining a reform of production and all culinary transformations, so as to guarantee, at any level, the sharing of the results and the pleasure. This path does not lead to a doctrine, but to the certainty that such a pleasure tacitly dominates all the others.

UTOPIA

Reproving the axiom attributed to Epicurus would be an academic challenge if we were not also talking about an association, an association involved in large-scale projects communicated in this almanac: farmers, markets, environment, biodiversity, communication networks. Like its branches, the roots of the tree are various and feed it in different ways. Could they perhaps interweave into a single point, that of pleasure? Responses can vary, imagining scales of value, hierarchies of objectives, pyramidal structures with a single bright point at the peak. But pleasure is not a supreme light; rather a fluid active in every moment of life, and that of the stomach, for its very ineluc-

TO DEFINE THE PLEASURE OF THE STOMACH IN TERMS OF 'WISDOM' IS TO TRANSCEND CONVIVIAL REFINEMENT;
IT IS TO SUBJECT THE BRAIN AND THOUGHT TO THE TEST OF THE SENSES.

MORAL BEAUTY
SENSORY GOODNESS

tability, for the sharing it demands, for the infinite variations that it assumes, whether by free choice or necessity, is the most diffused kind of pleasure. Many thinkers have written about utopian societies founded on pleasure. Brillat-Savarin's cousin, Charles Fourier, imagined one in which gastronomic and amorous passions were the pivot on which global social architectures were based. [2]

If a utopia becomes the inspiring principle of an association, we also find it in the way in which it imagines itself. The presidium, the convivium and the governorship obviously have nothing in common with Fourier's 'phalanxes', if not in the need to restore form to social structure, circulating new ideas and new principles, some of which are well-known to humanity but made sterile by their circumspect and circumscribed use.

Fourier was a utopian socialist, and his cousin a magistrate-gastronomist. How do we qualify those who, without being inspired by one or the other, work towards re-establishing economic systems starting from minuscule cultures, attracting the attention of the whole world to farmers, artisans and cooks and localizing the global instead of globalizing the local? What relationship do they have with pleasure? Any social project that eliminates it reproduces only the omnipotence of the tyrant-priest and forms of slavery; any association that integrates it becomes entirely pervaded by it, allowing the sprouting of new intellectual forms and their blossoming. There are energies created by the body, by desire, by thought and by all these together: without pleasure they extinguish themselves, because pleasure over-

turns values, reverses thoughts, confuses perceptions and makes the immediate future sustainable. Does the same happen with the pleasure of the stomach?

A BEAUTIFUL MORALITY

It is obviously a tautology that a gastronomic society is inspired by the pleasure of the stomach, subordinately integrating other pleasure categories, complementary and not absolute. But this response is again insufficient and tends to demonstrate that Epicurus must have been a gastronomist and not a philosopher, sitting at the table with his disciples and other sophists, in the moment in which he let fall: 'Spit on beautiful morality and on the idiot who admires anything which does not bring him pleasure.' [3]

This phrase goes well beyond the first, not for the way in which it was delivered nor for the violent reactions that it could (and does) provoke. If it admits the existence of a beautiful morality, of a consensus around virtuous actions—in current terms: some meditate on the hunger of others, others give money for food to those who ask for it—it radically denies a vicarious altruism which is the expression of an external mandate. Not only virtue and good are allies of pleasure, but they are subordinate to it to the extent that without it they have no effectiveness. Good must be planned by people and be their aim, and only if people assign it to themselves and their pleasure, can they operate *with* and *for* others. This is also easily applicable to gastronomic societies, which cannot be confused with workhouses, charitable schools and soup kitchens. For Slow Food, this means that there are no priests of Terra Madre nor guardians of the presidia nor hermits crouched at the base of the pear tree, the last example of its kind, and that all those who belong to it have assumed the responsibility of the pleasure of food and spit on its priesthood. But are we not putting in Epicurus's mouth a criticism of morality which has nothing in common with an association of gastronomists? Epicurus limited himself to providing a topic for discussion for contemporary and future dinner companions, without being responsible for the transferred use of his words. When we speak them, we take possession of a thought, without knowing it thoroughly, and it dilutes itself in our thought, so far away from Epicurus's. So what does it mean that I am an epicurean, if the words of Epicurus have now become our own?

NEW GASTRONOMY

The author of *The Deipnosophists*, where these two aphorisms can be found, comments on them, describing the persecution the epicureans would have suffered in Rome. This jump from philosophy to history introduces a third point of reflection. In the application of the philosophy of pleasure to Slow Food, the difficulty lies in making a principle of public morality of it, and as mentioned, a principle of food policy. The banquet of the gastronomists, seen from outside, is in fact similar to the dinner of the wealthy Epulon, and seems, in its public dimension, an excess to be hidden or criticized. The paradox of gastronomy therefore seems to be this: without pleasure, whether subjective or collective, it has no reason to exist, but elevating pleasure to the principle of the social function of gastronomy, it falls under the axe of censure or condemnation. How to escape from it? Certainly not with compromises that counterbalance morality and gastronomy, the good with the other good, or confine them in a sphere so exclusive as to seem private. The response of Slow Food to these doubts, which tend to minimize the significance of pleasure or to reduce its authority, has instead been to change the concept of gastronomy itself. Freed from conviviality as its only cultural celebration, strengthened by tools of knowledge and important objectives that reintroduce the principle of pleasure through the perception and description of the quality of products, gastronomy becomes the expression of the beautiful (moral) and the good (sensory). Athenaeus's Epicurus, obviously, plays no part, or, better, has, in a posthumous collection, provided the provocation of his two aphorisms and their radicalism to a debate, which, a few millennia later, no one intends to reopen. But in reality today the epicureans, instead of being persecuted, have been readmitted into Rome, with all the moral relativism of which they are capable.

Notes
1. Cited in Bertrand Russell, *History of Western Philosophy*, Routledge, 2004, p.233.
2. Charles Fourier, *Théorie des quatre mouvements – Le nouveau monde amoureux*, Dijon, Les presses du réel, 1998. In particular, the '*Gastronomie combinée envisagée en sens politique, matériel et passionné*' in the second part, pp. 270-282.
3. Cited in Giovanni Reale, translated by John R. Catan, *The Systems of the Hellenic Age: History of Ancient Philosophy*, SUNY Press, 1985, p.174.

WHY DRINK BIODYNAMIC WINES? ONLY AS A PHILOSOPHICAL ARGUMENT, FOR THE MORAL IMPERATIVE OF PROTECTING THE ENVIRONMENT? NO, THERE ARE MORE PROFOUND REASONS.

THE MUSIC OF THE SPHERES

Nicolas Joly
France, writer and viticulturist

PLEASURE

When an appraiser uncorks a bottle of wine, what does he look for? An emotion, a sense of completeness, inner satisfaction. He wants to discover or receive something that speaks to him, that delights him and promotes a cordial meeting that establishes itself at a table. In drinking a DOC (denomination-controlled) wine, one intends to establish a relationship with a place, to taste the life within it. To call it DOC is to speak of an original taste, a taste linked to a vine. But this taste originates from a specific region, from the entire life of a place, from the landscape, the fauna, the climate—elements that participate, discreetly yet strongly, in the taste that the grapevine collects and concentrates within its grapes: the minute particularities of the climate, absorbed by the vine through its leaves with photosynthesis, and of the soil, appropriated by its roots with the help of microorganisms.

Let us not forget that the mass of material—tons per hectare that the vine produces between the beginning of spring, after a pruning that leaves just the smallest gems, and autumn—is made 95 percent from solar energy, light that the vine transforms into matter, captures in cellulose, starch, sugar. Only 5 percent of the material comes from the soil. The intangible, the 'non-material' is made tangible. All the taste of a wine—its nose, aromas, body, structure—is essentially 'celestial' material that the vine has laboriously converted into something concrete, accessible to our senses. If with irresponsible acts, counseled by all the schools of agriculture, one uses herbicides that kill all life in the soil, systemic treatments that poison the water, that represent for the vines the only possible link to the solar world, and in fact all the extensive work done by the vines is countered—in certain cases completely destroyed it. At that point it becomes necessary—to the end of satisfying, even in an improper way, the wine assessor— running back to artificial technologies that can recreate, arbitrarily, alluring tastes that are foreign to what the region is capable of offering. Certainly, what comes out is a 'good' wine; nevertheless, we can tell something is off. We are alerted to a sort of latent dissastisfaction; we feel that there isn't something living in there. You could say that the music that the wine should play is absent, that the soul of the winemaker isn't there. You don't feel as captured, warmed up, healed—given that real wine has certain therapeutic effects—as you would from a delicate, subtle, long-lived and balanced expression that could almost be compared to the contemplation of a work of art or a great landscape.

UNDERSTANDING THE EARTH

In organic agriculture, substantial progress has been made. The aim is to allow nature to express herself without antagonizing her with terrible poisons or synthetics, which are at times so dangerous that people who apply them must put on masks to breathe and airtight suits. The hidden system that supports life on Earth and that is articulated by realms of the living should not be disturbed.

In organic agriculture, more must be done. We need to understand the matrix of life—without which the Earth would be a cadaver—to make it stronger. Above all, we need to understand that the Earth is linked to a solar system by frequency and wavelength. Light, colors and sounds are not these! That sun we miss so much when it's not there doesn't touch us in a tangible, material way, even as much as we appreciate its effects! We must rediscover intangible life: it isn't made of impulses, of rhythms composed by an addition of frequencies and wavelengths. When an animal dies we don't see anything exhaled from its body. Too often that which we call life is not the same as the effects of life on the physical world.

This rather cursory explanation can perhaps help us better understand why biodynamic

C. ORR/AR/CORBIS

agriculture uses just a few grams or a few hundred grams per hectare of various soil preparations, all natural. These preparations uniquely take effect by connectors, by receptors of those very specific vital processes the plant needs to best express itself on the physical plane. In biodynamics there are no substitutions made to impose material behavior (chemical fertilization, for example, that forces growth, requiring more water than necessary); it doesn't violate the vine, as with genetic engineering, but is instead limited to helping it better carry out its work. The vines are put in tune with archetypal forces, the solar, planetary and stellar forces that the plant fundamentally needs to completely express the complexity of a DOC. In this way, the work of a winery is very simple. All the vital processes present in the grape allow its juice to become wine virtually by itself.

HARMONIES THAT SHAPE

Let's go a little deeper. If the Earth became enveloped in an enormous piece of black plastic, just about every life form on the planet would cease to exist. Everyone just about everywhere talks these days about the evil effects of CO_2, but never of the enormous energy pollution that increasingly weakens the Earth every day. I think of all the arbitrary wavelengths and frequencies with which man saturates the atmosphere through his numerous satellites, GPS, cellular telephones, TV, radar, without understanding the interference created by them, ranging from extra-low frequencies (ELF) to gigahertz for cellphones (900 to 1800 billion vibrations per second), within the energy matrix present in the atmosphere from which we receive our vital forces. It is the entire energy organism that gives life to the Earth that is being destroyed today. All these harmonies—what our ancestors called 'music of the spheres'—that give shape to material

and become plants, animals or human beings come from an incredibly active energy
system, a system that, without support,
organizes, separates and unites atoms,
forming the immense diversity of the living world that surrounds us. Ultimately, as
the Nobel Prize winner in physics Maxwell
Planck said, all the physical dimension in
its great diversity is not a mass of atoms
in perennial agitation condensed by ter-
restrial gravity. The continuous movement,
that we define as frequencies, was called
by our ancestors 'vibrations'. We can then
deeply understand why biodynamics has
so many effects on the taste of wine: it acts
on the vibratory world before transforming
the material one. Biodynamics puts the
soil and the plant in tune with that which
gives them life. To think that genes are the
only things responsible for this work is not
reasonable, as much as thinking that the
TV presenter lives inside the television set.
Genes are not fundamentally the emitters/
receivers.

KNOWLEDGE

Why speak of all these things in an article
on biodynamic wine? Because it helps to
understand that, thanks to biodynamics,
even only with partial comprehension of
the impulses conferred upon plants by
the sun, the planets, the constellations
(astronomy is not the same thing as as-
trology), these forces can be used in agriculture. It can serve this system gratis,

IN ORGANIC AGRICULTURE, THE AIM IS TO ALLOW NATURE TO EXPRESS HERSELF WITHOUT ANTAGONIZING HER WITH TERRIBLE POISONS OR SYNTHETIC

reinforcing expression in the vine in every way, if that's what's desired. Biodynamics, in the final analysis, is the result of an immense body of knowledge that has allowed the construction of sacred places like cathedrals, temples and pyramids; that shows us how to harness specific energies that can in certain cases be used to heal man (alternative medicine). Through biodynamics, the agricultural industry will once again become an art, thanks to man's ability to link different energies to the plant. We'll no longer be dealing with an art in terms of the mineral plane and that which it makes concrete, an architecture well understood, in majestic internal forms that can give a sense of elevation, but an art on the holistic plane. Which impulses provide—and to which plants—the desired effects? This is the apprenticeship that the new generation must complete by themselves, as there is virtually no established school in that sense. A wine produced biodynamically, if this method is comprehensive, well applied, well adapted to the place and to the vine, is like immensely profound music—like a song that resonates in the perfect acoustics of a place in which the polarity of stones and law of numbers is respected. It is a moment in which to be reconciled with the world. Comprehension of it will perhaps allow a few of us to rediscover the subtle flavors that a plant or animal can offer, if treated with respect and understanding, and not with a knowledge made up only of neurons.

MOLECULES, AT TIMES SO DANGEROUS THAT PEOPLE WHO APPLY THEM MUST PUT ON MASKS TO BREATHE AND AIRTIGHT SUITS.

E. LESSING, MAGNUM/CONTRASTO

I DRINK ALONE

Michel Smith
France, journalist and writer

PLEASURE

The scene takes place in my family doctor's surgery. Twisting and turning on my chair in front of his imposing desk, finally, despite my terrible embarrassment, I start speaking. I must say that in circumstances such as these, I often find my courage deserting me.

'Dr. Bacchus, I've come to you because I've decided to cure myself.'

'Good. What seems to be the problem?'

'For some years I've found myself preferring cold wines.'

'And what do you mean by this?'

'How can I explain? For me, wine at room temperature is finished. It's over. Whites, rosés, reds—it doesn't matter, I don't like my wines any more unless they're between 8 and 14 degrees C.'

'And so?'

'In society everyone points me out for public ridicule. In restaurants the sommelier acts like a prosecutor. I feel guilty of some unknown lese-majesty crime. And when having dinner with friends I'm reduced to drinking water or asking for a beer. Everyone stares. I feel like the whole world has a grudge against me. Listen, the other day at my local wine bar, which was particularly overheated, I asked for a nice bucket three-quarters full of cold water with just a handful of ice cubes for a bottle of my favorite Pauillac—you know, the Château Ponete-Canet. I got insulted for this! I was shame personified.'

'And so?'

'So...now I don't go out any more: to top it all, I drink alone. I pour a well-chilled wine into a large glass and watch talk shows on TV, imagining that I'm among 'normal' guests, people who don't shoot me withering looks. Drinking alone ... do you realize the gravity of my situation? Please, I beg you, do something.'

'I understand. I'm sending you for a brief stay with Alcoholics Anonymous until you're back to normal. In the meantime, I'm prescribing five glasses of warm Coca-Cola a day. That should put your taste buds back in order.'

HEAT AND TANNINS

That's when I woke up. Drenched in sweat, totally panicked, my mouth as dry as an oversalted prosciutto that's been hung too long. Throwing myself on a large glass of tap water, I trembled like a dead leaf in an autumn wind. How could I have invented such a story in my subconscious? Although... Warm fizzy drinks I'd already tried. I was in a remote oasis deep in the Mauritanian desert, I believe it was Chinguetti, in the shade of an old wall made of

WINE
RIGHT TEMPERATURE

stones, straw and mud that the French army had built in an attempt to securely establish their illusory colonial conquest. At the time, I didn't dare drink water for fear of traveler's dysentery. And in effect the dark, foamy soda seemed to cure my thirst. But five minutes later, perhaps because of the poor quality of the citric acid which seemed to be the only important ingredient in that Marlboro-smokers' drink, I found my throat as dry as before. I had no choice but to turn to the local green tea. A boiling drink to placate my thirst... really, I thought I'd seen it all! Since then I've learned that Chinese tea contains more than one thing that's good for the health: tannins, for example, and vitamin C. That's why tea has always been one of my favorite drinks, after wine of course. I can even go so far as to find in it a certain thirst-quenching freshness. Since that episode, the idea of freshness has been decisive in my critical and sensory approach to wine.

REASONABLE REFUSALS

If hot tea can be thirst-quenching, hot wine is instead only good for soothing fevers and producing sweat. Well, by now you'll have grasped that for some time I've been engaged on a crusade to defend the correct temperature for wine at all costs. What can I say, I love chilled wines! But even when I do my best, being as polite as possible so that the wine will be served at 'my' temperature, they still always bring it too warm for my tastes. That's why now I order it cold, relying on the old adage: 'At the table it's easier to heat up a cold wine than to cool down a warm wine.' But I can assure you that my struggle is long and arduous. I run into a significant amount of resistance, as stupid as it is archaic. 'But sir, a Bordeaux should be served at room temperature, and I can promise you that ours is no warmer than 20-22 degrees.' By now everyone knows that the expression 'room temperature' was invented at a time when wine was brought up from a cold cellar to rooms without central heating never over 20 degrees C. Some extremists even went so far as to practice the perversion of putting the bottle in front of the fireplace! I am so sick and tired of this willful non-comprehension of something that seems to flow directly from common sense, that sometimes I even give up. And then I resign myself to simply refusing to drink a warm wine, even when I'm not paying. What tactlessness! But how to convince a sommelier whose school did not teach 'the right temperature of wine' that my refusal is eminently reasonable? How to explain that I am a customer and that the customer has the right to feel like a king for an evening? If by a stroke of good luck I find one who, in response to my simple request 'Can you put that Oregon Pinot Noir in a bucket of water with a little ice'? immediately says 'Yes sir, no problem,' then I sing—in my mind—the praises of all the gods of wine. If the bottle arrives in cold water up to its neck, or if the decanter is brought in an ice bucket, then I am ready to get up from the table and embrace the sommelier. But if by misfortune he takes it into his head to serve

BY NOW YOU'LL HAVE GRASPED THAT FOR SOME TIME I'VE BEEN ENGAGED ON A CRUSADE TO DEFEND THE CORRECT TEMPERATURE FOR WINE AT ALL COSTS.

H. CARTIER-BRESSON, MAGNUM/CONTRASTO

MAKERS AND TASTERS

me the bottle in a small bucket, with water that barely covers the base, then in the face of such disloyalty I will fly into a rage. My dinner will be ruined and I will cry scandal. If the wine offered to me exceeds 18 degrees in a dining room so hot that shirtsleeves are called for—without mentioning the glass, whose sides are also warm—is it not perhaps the sommelier's duty to suggest keeping the wine cool? And how is this done? From experience, I know that a bottle maintains the correct temperature when placed in a bucket full of cold water with two or three ice cubes, which can replaced during the meal as necessary. Why do they not teach these things at sommelier school? Don't be surprised if one day a sommelier is killed during service. Notify the police: it will have been me! That said, please don't think I really hate the profession of sommelier quite that much. It's just that I can't bring myself to accept the massacre of that pleasure I find in discovering the wine of my dreams.

PERFECTION AT 12°C

In some ways the winemakers must also take the blame. Among them there is a sect of admirers of warm wine, to the point that we have to ask if they really do love their wines. At a recent visit to the Vinisud show in Montpellier, all the Mediterranean reds, some of which were quite noteworthy, were already undrinkable by the end of the morning, with the overheated environment causing their alcohol to stand out instead of their fresh-

ness. The exhibition's organizers even made ice available, but it was sparingly used only to chill the whites. The same thing often happens at the great international wine fair Vinexpo, held in Bordeaux. Only certain great chateaux were attentive enough to bring us into their air-conditioned spaces. Result: no one can think about drinking anything but water. In contrast, if there is one professional fair I would recommend it is that held in Angers in the Loire Valley, which opens at the start of the winter. In my opinion, it is one of the best fairs in the world. Here the winemakers are used to drinking their wines at cellar temperatures. More often than not these cellars are carved deep into the chalky rock, and their temperature never rises above 12 degrees C, even in the summer. Often, for whites as well as reds, initiates—first of all the winemakers—hold the wine glass cupped tightly in their hands for a few minutes, warming it before taking the first sip. As a result in Vouvray, Chinon and Savennières the wines are always chilled, which not only enhances their grace but also their natural acidity, inspiring connoisseurs to drink them gladly. On the other hand, I get very irritated when the sommelier arrives with a bottle of Chablis Grand Cru close to 0 degrees, when it should have at least 10 more; or when winemakers in Burgundy or elsewhere have me taste a white that has spent the night in a refrigerator set to the coldest setting. Just like tropical heat, near-polar cold is unbearable when you are trying to get to know the soul of a wine.

145

M. SAROLDI/PHO-TO

S. SERRA/PHO-TO

M. SAROLDI/PHO-TO

EATING UP CULTURE

Matthew Fort
United Kingdom, journalist and writer

PLEASURE

Come with me. Climb up the steps of this shack on stilts on the beach at Tangalle in Sir Lanka. Sit down on one of the mismatched plastic chairs and tuck you knees under the rickety table, covered with a lurid sail cloth. Ah, the view, the shifting, twinkling, azure Indian Ocean in front, palm trees bent to the wind to either side. Ah, the food—kakuluwo—crab curry, with a plate of plain rice on the side and a mango to follow. Pick up the crab in your fingers, and bite through its carapace, crunching down, releasing delicate shellfish sweetness through the rippling chilli heat, with its hum of ginger, garlic, turmeric, fenugreek, cinnamon, the sourness of curry leaves. A forkful of rice, a sip of iced beer...

Isn't this why we travel, really, truthfully? When each mouthful reminds us that we are somewhere else and sends a shiver of pleasure through the brain, locking flavour and sensation firmly away in our memory.

They say that travel broadens the mind. In my experience it tends to broaden every other part of the anatomy as well. That may be because food is at the heart of travel. It is why we travel, even if we don't think about it, because food is the distillation of another people's culture. It is its history on a plate. It is the living embodiment of a country's past and present. It is the point at which any traveller meets the people of the land in which he or she is travelling.

Museums, monuments, temples and treasures are all fine in their way, but they are fixed points. They make statements about a place at a specific time. Only food (and language) continues to evolve century after century, weaving an edible tapestry from ingredients introduced at this time or that, making use of techniques that recall the influence of a wave of immigration, conquest or social change.

CENTURIES OF SWEET AND SOUR

Anyone who has visited Sicily will be aware of the ubiquity of *caponata*. There's isn't an antipasto served on that island that doesn't have a blob of that vegetable stew. Usually, but not invariably, aubergines, celery, onion, tomato sauce, capers and olives. Its defining quality is that it is *agrodolce*—sour and sweet.

I say 'almost invariably' because there are as many versions of *caponata* as there are cooks. You can find *caponata* without celery, a heresy to some, without tomato sauce, and, oddity to others, without capers, without olives. You can find caponata with slivers of almond, nibs of chocolate, tentacles of squid, dotted with raisins. You can eat deep, sonorous mulchy *caponata*, and *caponata* as light on their feet as Ginger Rogers & Fred Astaire and of every weight and complexion in between. But if you take the orthodox *caponata* outlined above—aubergines, celery, onions, tomatoes, capers, olives, vinegar, sugar, and olive oil—deconstruct it and examine its parts, you will see that through it you can read at least part of the extraordinary history of the extraordinary island of Sicily.

The aubergine began its life as a wild fruit in India and made its way to the Mediterranean via Turkey, a testament to ancient trade roots. It was introduced to Sicily by the Moors, who ruled the island from 831 AD until 1091. Celery is indigenous to the island. Indeed, Selinunte, with its great temples, takes its name from *selinon*, the Greek for celery. Of course, Sicily was part of Magna Graecia—the richest part of Magna Graecia—between the mid-7th century BC until 212 BC or so. Then it was the turn of the Romans. What did they bring to the *caponata*? The taste for sweet-sour things, perhaps. Apicius lists several *agrodolce* dishes (*porcellum coriandratum*, pork with coriander, and *piscibus elixis*, sauce for poaching fish) in *De Re Coquinaria*—though you could argue that the Arab taste for using honey and fruit in dishes started off the fashion. Or maybe it was the medical theories of the second-century Greek physician, Galen, and his theory of humours. In short, you could argue over the origins of *agrodolce* until you died of old age. Whatever the truth, and there probably isn't a final, definitive one, vinegar has been round since men started making alcohol, because booze has always gone off as a result of being naturally invaded by certain bacteria which turn the alcohol into acetic acid. The Babylonians were certainly making vinegar in 4000 BC.

Nowadays, while we prefer a bit of consistency and control rather than leaving things to nature, we still use vinegar in much the same way and for much the same reasons as the Babylonians did, as a preservative and a palate sharpener. For sweetening, the Romans used honey. The Moors introduced sugar cane to Sicily, but the universal use of sugar had to wait until the 19th century, when Franz Archard perfected the means of making sugar out of sugar beet. What's left? Oh yes, tomatoes. Well, we all know that they came to Europe from the Americas (along with capsicums, corn, potatoes, tobacco, turkeys and chocolate) at a time when Sicily was part of the Spanish empire. (In return we gave them smallpox and horses.)

CULTURAL DIGEST

So there you have it. When you eat *caponata*, whether in Marsala or Messina, Palermo or Pachino, you are eating several millennia of Sicilian history, all together at the same time. 'Time present and time past/Are both perhaps present in time future,/And time future contained in time past,' as T. S. Eliot put it in *The Four Quartets*. He should have also said that past, present and future are all contained in food.

FOOD
AND IDENTITY

The same is true of any country. Food never arrives on the plate by accident. There is always a story and history behind even the simplest and apparently most casual dishes. Even in Britain, where we have been guilty of acting as if we are ashamed of our own food and adopted that of other countries wholesale. But should some curious visitor to our shores be peering in a bakery or tea shop window around Easter, he or she will come across the hot-cross bun, sweet and spicy, made of leavened dough and currants, with a creamy cross on its glossy top, traditionally served on Good Friday. The religious significance of the cross is obvious, but the use of yeast refers to the country's brewing tradition—brewer's yeast used to be widely used. The currants speak of trade with the Mediterranean, or possibly Britain's Roman past. The spices—cinnamon, nutmeg, mace—bring the whiff of the Far East, the history of the spice trade. Sliced open, toasted and spread with butter ... we can begin another monograph on Britain's dairy industry. Top the butter with jam, and we have the whole fascinating field of fruit varieties, preserving and the economics of sugar production. Of course, that's not how most of us approach the business of eating when we go abroad. We stop at a street stall, pop into a bar, sit down at table in a restaurant because we are hungry, because we are curious. We approach the menu (assuming there is one), or listen to the list of dishes reeled off to us in a language we probably don't understand very well or peer at unfamiliar ingredients bubbling away in a steamy cauldron with a mixture of trepidation mixed with excitement. It's quite different from the kind of excitement we might feel when we visit museums or monuments, temples or treasures. Then we encounter another culture in an inert, sanitised form. This is the past. It is controllable, comfortable. We stand outside it. Even when we travel within a country, we are insulated to a greater or lesser degree by the means of transport we choose, the insularity of language, and the group, large or small, with which we are travelling. It is only when we eat that we engage that culture in its true, vivid, living state. Assuming, that is, we haven't dashed off to the nearest McDonalds or Starbucks, or locked ourselves away in the comfort zone of our hotel. That is why the protection and promotion of each country's culinary culture is of such critical importance. Peoples' deepest sense of identity lies in their food. It's curious that immigrants lose their clothes, social habits, language, religion even, before they lose their taste for the food of their country of origin. It is one of the ironies of food in America, for example, that all those dishes with which we associate the grossest forms of the nation's gastronomic and capitalist imperialism—hamburger, hot dog, pizza, taco— started off life as the dishes of respective impoverished immigrant peoples. They just followed the parabola of the American dream, and became immensely rich. The pleasure and joy of life lie in its diversity and variety, not in homogeneity. Why bother to travel to other places, if they aren't different from the place where we live. Food is the embodiment of that difference, presented in its most accessible, most pleasurable (usually) form. The English poet John Keats wrote 'Much have I travell'd in the realms of gold,/And many goodly states and kingdoms seen'. Just substitute the word 'food' for gold. It's more interesting, enduring and, in the final analysis, more valuable.

Caffè
di Huehuetenango

TO APPRECIATE A FOOD, IT IS IMPORTANT TO KNOW ABOUT ITS SOCIAL AND CULTURAL

SIGNIFICANCE, ITS GEOGRAPHICAL CONTEXT AND PRODUCTION METHODS ARE ALSO IMPORTANT.

Three bees for a spoonful of honey

Narita Shigeyuki
Japan, vice-president of Slow Food Japan
Photos Alberto Peroli

EDUCATION

Japanese Slow Food members had their first taste of the Master of Food course at the 2004 Salone del Gusto. The encounter had an immediate effect: once back home, there were vociferous calls for the educational program to be launched in our

own country. So we produced the first Master of Food in Japan with the help of two teachers from the Italian version, Gianni Pistrini and Lorenzo Lazzarini. Initially we were unsure of what topics to cover, as Japan already has plenty of courses on well-known products like wine and cheese. We decided to concentrate on foods that were popular but not so commonly studied, and which would lend themselves to comparisons between Italy and Japan. In the end we settled on coffee and honey.

The first demonstration lessons were held in July 2007, first in Tokyo and then in other regions around Japan. The theme of the inaugural evening was a comparison between coffee roasting at the Le Vallette prison in Turin, run by the Pausa Café cooperative, and honey production in Ginza, one of Tokyo's chicest neighborhoods. The presentation of the Piedmontese project caused a great stir; everyone wanted to know why the prison was chosen, what kind of coffee was roasted, where it came from—and of course they wanted to taste it as well.

The story of Ginza honey also inspired great interest. The bees are kept on the roofs of neighborhood buildings and collect pollen from parks, the imperial gardens and trees lining the surrounding streets, with the resulting honey used by some of Tokyo's best-known confectioners. The project is linked to a movement fighting for improved environmental quality in Ginza and the promotion of local products.

ESPRESSO FOREVER

The lesson on coffee was held by Gianni Pistrini. He started by showing a photo of a coffee flower, and it felt almost as though its fragrance was spreading through the room. Pistrini's teaching technique was excellent. Using a series of illustrations he outlined the history and culture of coffee up to its current popularity around the world. Then the tast-

MEMBERS OF THE PAUSA CAFÉ' COOPERATIVE AND INMATES WHO ROAST COFFEE IN THE TURIN PRISON.

ings let everyone experience for themselves the characteristics and differences between the arabica and robusta varieties. Variations in the beans, roasting methods, water and pouring techniques all produced such different results, it was almost hard to believe it was the same beverage. After each tasting, the participants filled out an evaluation form with their impressions.

Tsuneo Nakazawa, the leading local coffee roaster, also took part in the Master, leading a comparative tasting between Japanese and Italian coffees.

However the class's primary object of interest was espresso. Many Japanese don't know espresso, or think it isn't good even if they've never tried it. Using an Italian machine we had the chance to taste a 'real' espresso and Gianni's explanations helped us appreciate its quality. Many people fell in love and vowed never to drink American-style coffee again. Such was the enthusiasm that at the end of the lesson someone suggested going straight to Turin to sample a Pausa Café espresso.

NECTAR OF THE GODS

Lorenzo Lazzarini led the honey lesson, explaining the link between flowers, insects, the climate and the environment. His words recalled Darwin's theory of evolution and Fabre's *Souvenirs entomologiques* as he illustrated the differences between European and Japanese bees, the distinctive features of pollen from different flowers and how it is collected and transformed into honey. The tasting of six kinds of honey included two Presidia honeys, two Italian organic honeys and two Japanese honeys. Again the participants filled out a form with their evaluations, and exchanged opinions about the differences between the products. We Japanese are not very good at expressing sensations, but Lorenzo helped us with the advice to 'sense' not just with the tongue and the nose, but also with the mind and the whole body.

Seita Fujiwara, head of the beekeeping family that runs the Ginza honey project, presented Japanese honey. The class found it to be more delicate than Italian, with the differences in fragrance reflecting and helping to understand the differences between Japanese and Italian cultures.

Everyone was excited to put their new knowledge into practice. When one housewife heard that it takes the ceaseless life's work of three bees to make just one spoonful of honey, she decided that in the future she would give it a more important role in the kitchen, rather than simply spreading it on bread.

GREEN TEA AND SOBA

Around 300 participants took part in the lessons, and they came from diverse backgrounds: nutritionists, cooks, cooking school instructors, coffee sellers, housewives and students from all over the country. The choice of the two subjects, honey and coffee, proved very popular. Though consumed every day, in general we know very little about them.

Japan has many specialized institutions that organize specific programs, but the Master of Food offers something different, a multi-faceted course that covers a product's history, culture, production methods and tasting techniques. The teaching style, which places the students at the center, is also innovative. Giving importance to what the participants are sensing and their opinions is very different from the Japanese 'one-way' method, centered on the teacher.

It's now time for Japan to take another step forward, and in fall 2008 we plan to inaugurate a truly Japanese version of the program, starting with green tea and buckwheat soba noodles, and expanding in the future to cover sake, soy sauce and miso (fermented soy beans). Once again I hope to count on the support of all the Italian staff, and who knows, maybe in the future it will be our teachers coming to Italy to lead demonstrations and tastings!

THERE ISN'T A HIGH CUISINE AND A LOW CUISINE, THERE'S JUST CUISINE OF THE PEOPLE.
AND TIME FOR CULTURES TO INTERACT.

NO JOB FOR ARCHAEOLOGISTS

José N. Iturriaga de la Fuente
Mexico, writer and winner of the Slow Food Award for the Defense
of Biodiversity in 2003
Photos Nino Leto

TRADITION

The study of traditions is mainly a subject for anthropologists and there are two opposing positions one can adopt, which can be illustrated by using two popular aphorisms. The first one sounds the refrain 'Change or die', while the second states that 'Traditions shouldn't be touched even with a rose petal'. All extreme positions end up being in the wrong: an Aristotelian happy medium is the most desirable and sensible attitude.

One also needs to consider that any tradition, however old it might be, has after all originated at a particular moment, or rather has emerged during a specific period. The question of food traditions is a useful example and Slow Food knows this very well. We can look at the case of Mexico, which has analogies in most countries of the world.

Present-day Mexican cuisine is a hybrid cuisine deriving from a mixture of pre-Columbian indigenous elements with Hispanic elements, which began to combine from the time of the conquest of Mexico. The Hispanic elements in turn included a store of foods and methods which originated not only in Spain, but other areas of Europe and even other continents; this is the case of spices from the Far East and various products from Asia Minor or North Africa which blended into Spanish culinary traditions.

So it would be wrong to claim that today in 21st-century Mexico there is a traditional pre-Columbian cuisine. No stew or other present-day dish was devised according to pure indigenous tradition before the arrival of the Spanish in the 16th century.

TACO AND TORTILLAS
Hybridization and cross-fertilization enhance and enrich. Ancient Mexican food traditions—

A VERY OLD VERSION OF TACOS FILLED WITH LARVAE FROM *MAGUEY* AGAVES IS STILL PRODUCED TODAY WITH THE ANCIENT CORN *TORTILLA*.

MESTIZO
CUISINE

forcefully coming back into fashion nowadays—are equally suited for native products (such as corn, beans, peppers, tomatoes, avocado, chocolate or turkey) and for other products from overseas (rice, cinnamon, coconut, mango, Asian tamarind, weak, peaks, onions, or chicken—from Europe—and Arabic sesame).

Pre-Columbian Mexican cuisine has thus been enriched as a result of the Spanish conquest, incorporating pork and pig fat, cheese and cream, meat from cattle, sheep or goats. For centuries it would be inconceivable to think of traditional Mexican cuisine without products from overseas. A very old version of *tacos* filled with larvae from *maguey* agaves is still produced today with the ancient corn *tortilla*; but the corn is prepared using slaked lime instead of limestone, and the dough is no longer spread by hand but with a *tortilla* press; finally, the larvae are no longer roasted but fried. This is just one of many examples that could be cited.

So reviving and defending traditions does not mean resurrecting extinct historical customs and traditions; it is not archaeology. If you want to revive traditions, defend, promote and spread them, you have to accept the fact that cultures blend together and with

the passing of centuries they end up intermingled, giving life to new cultures. In the case of Mexico, it is not a question of reviving Aztec or Olmec traditions, which for a long time have belonged to ancient history, but of protecting popular traditions which due to their ancient roots, definitely define Mexican cultural and food character.

ANTI-CULTURE

Accepting that the merging of cultures is inevitable, even if not desirable (as happened for Greece and Rome, giving rise to Greco-Roman culture, the foundation of present-day western culture) does not mean passively accepting (and certainly not with open arms) the invasions carried out by industrialized economies, which not only attack local economies but also local cultures.

Hamburgers, with all that they represent, are certainly not culture. Rather they are anti-culture, because they do not create something new through cross-fertilization, but tend to destroy through subjection.

When the first university on the American continent was founded in Mexico towards the middle of the 16th century, bison were grazing in Washington. So as far as culture

MEXICAN CUISINE IS AN ELEMENT OF SOCIAL COHESION INVOLVING ALL LEVELS OF SOCIETY. IT IS ONE OF THE MOST POWERFUL CONTRIBUTORS TO NATIONAL IDENTITY, COMPARABLE TO THE VIRGIN OF GUADALUPE.

THERE ISN'T A MEXICAN 'HAUTE CUISINE'. ACCEPTING ITS EXISTENCE WOULD MEAN THERE IS ALSO A 'LOW CUISINE', AND THAT IS NOT THE CASE.

TYPICAL INGREDIENTS

is concerned, particularly gastronomic culture, the most effective defense of our national frontiers against the chaos of globalization is the strength of our cultural traditions.

It should also be added that a people's most deep-rooted traditions are spread throughout all social classes: they rise from the mass of ordinary people to the elite, they extend from the bottom of the social pyramid to the top. This is the case for Mexican cuisine and it is certainly typical of the situation found around the world.

So there isn't a Mexican 'haute cuisine'. Accepting its existence would mean there is also a 'low cuisine', and that is not the case. Traditional Mexican cuisine, which people have maintained since the time of our grandparents and further back still, is the same as can be found on the sumptuous tables of the rich, in private houses and restaurants. Authentic Mexican high cuisine is in fact the traditional cuisine of ordinary people. Another very different matter is the modern fashion—whether good or bad—of fusion cuisine, celebrity cuisine or *nouvelle cuisine*, which may use typical Mexican ingredients, but prepared in a non-traditional way. Mexican high cuisine is based on the traditions of the people.

There are excellent five-star restaurants offering traditional Mexican cuisine.

ROOTS

The gastronomic traditions of a people are not just managed in the kitchen and do not only involve diet or nutrition. Their roots are buried in history, religion, rituals, anthropology and sociology. In Mexico they involve the graves of the dead and the cradles of babies; they are a matrix of ancient knowledge enriched through the many stages of cross-fertilization. They appear in temples and altars, inspire propitiatory dances, merge with the cycle of life, can be found in prayers and decorate the cemeteries. They form a cultural whole which embodies community and family practices.

Mexican cuisine is an element of social cohesion involving all levels of society. It is one of the most powerful contributors to national identity, comparable to the Virgin of Guadalupe. Mexico is not an exception. The Slow Food movement has grown so dramatically because there are traditional cuisines and food traditions in all countries of the world: it is our duty to save, defend, promote and spread them so the distinctive cultural character of different people around the world does not wither away.

ABOVE, ABRAHAM AND THE SACRIFICE OF ISAAC, BYZANTINE MOSAIC (540 AD C.), BASILICA OF SAN VITALE, RAVENNA.
BELOW: NOAH INEBRIATED, (12TH CENTURY), PALATINE CHAPEL, PALERMO.

PESACH DINNER

Moshe Basson
Israel (of Iraqi origin). A member of the Chefs for Peace association of 25 Arabs and Israelis: Jews, Muslims and Christians

TRADITION

The Hebrew word for tradition, cited in the scriptures and the earliest addenda to them, symbolizes passing on (from hand to hand) or by word of mouth. The English word 'tradition' comes from the Latin *tradere*, also meaning to delivery or hand over. Defining tradition from where I stand, I tremble a little and feel somewhat mystified. I find myself drifting to a whirlpool of memories of tastes and aromas, sounds, words and letters in several languages. Writing about tradition isn't as simple as it seems. The food that I cook in my restaurant, eat at my home—my mother's casseroles, my own casseroles—and anywhere else is traditional food.

When it comes to religion, I define myself as an observing Jew, a traditional Jew. I even cultivate my little garden traditionally.

EXODUS

As I type out t -r -a -d -i -t -i -o -n on the keyboard, I feel a sense of vertigo, as if I was flying through different dimensions, far from one other, but all of them in the present. I am with the Israelites as they flee from Egypt past Mount Sinai. I feel like Moses, who hasn't eaten for 40 days and 40 nights on the mountain. I stand there, scenting the aroma of the broiled lamb of the sacrifice of the Passover: the Paschal lamb, eaten with matzos and bitter herbs.

At the same time, I'm sitting at table of my father, blessed be his soul, on the Passover Seder. The scent of the four glasses of homemade wine, which we are commanded to drink on this holiday, blends with the aroma of dates, honey, *silan*, which this evening accompanies crisp, bitterish hearts of lettuce, chopped walnuts and unleavened bread. On waves of taste and scent and sound, there on Mount Sinai, I am carried further through the pages of the Book of Genesis to the story of the Garden of Eden.

Out of the ground the Lord God caused to grow every tree that is pleasing to the sight and good for food.

And where is the apple...?

Its perfume caresses my nostrils and my eyes open like those of Adam and Eve after tasting it.

And the eyes of them both were opened, and they knew that they were naked.

Genesis Chapter 3:7

I walk in the garden of the days of yore, the blood of Abel is saturated in its soil. Abel, the shepherd who was murdered by his farmer brother Cain. And there on the same ground after the big flood, stands Noah, a little tipsy, establishing a new civilization, its culture partly founded on the making and drinking of wine.

And Noah the husbandman began, and planted a vineyard, And he drank of the wine, and was drunken...
Genesis Chapter 9: 20-21

All of them are in the garden, Abraham the Hebrew and his sons Ishmael and Isaac. Ishmael sits hungry and thirsty in the arms of Hagar, his mother, under a sage plant. Isaac smells the ram broiled on the impromptu altar on Mount Moriah. A moment ago he was bound to the altar. In his old age when he is blind and only scents stimulate his memories, Isaac lusts for the savory flavors of broiled game. He asks his son Esau to hunt game for him. And Esau, bewildered by the aroma of the lentil stew that his brother Jacob has cooked, brings home no game and is tricked into giving up his birthright.

AUNTIE ZEINAB

The intoxicating aroma of lentil stew takes me to the Arab village of Beit Safafa near Jerusalem. To our family bakery in the 1960s. I'm a little boy and this time the aroma is that of *shourbat aadds*, an Arab lentil soup that Zeinab, our Arab neighbor, cooks. Zeinab is like an aunt for me. I call her Auntie Zeinab to this day.

In a relatively modern bakery they make a traditional bread. Iraqi flat pitas baked stuck to the sides of the walls of a clay stove, like a huge pitcher with a fire inside. The stove has a round opening in the front of its upper section; through that opening, my uncle Nazem enters his hand holding a round cushion with the pita dough. In a split second, he pastes it on the inner walls of the stove of clay.

... and the priest shall offer the whole, and make it smoke upon the altar; it is a burnt offering, an offering made by fire, of a sweet savor unto the Lord.
Leviticus Chapter 1: 13

From the chimneys of the bakery other scents are rising. Those of traditional Arab pastries, like *kras* (dumplings filled with fresh hyssop leaves, sumac and lots of springtime green onion shoots), those of *lachma be-ag'in*, that my Muslim aunt Zeinab makes. She came from a village which, before 1967, before the territory was divided, was half in Jordan and half in Israel.

The colors and aromas and noises of the Arab boys of the neighborhood on their holiday. I'm reminded again of Moses, of Mount Sinai. *Thou shalt not kill. Thou shalt not steal. Remember the Sabbath day, to keep it holy ... You will not eradicate fire on the seventh day... Thou shalt not seethe a kid in its mother's milk ... From this and from that you will eat and from this and that you will not eat, as it is a detestation and untouchable for thee.*
Exodus Chapter 23 (19)

And like Moses who sees the Promised Land but cannot enter, I see, smell and feel. I can even hear the foods and savory dishes as my Auntie Zeinab prepares them, but I cannot consume them. Those savory dishes cooked in a separate stove in my father's bakery are not kosher, which means I cannot eat them. Though, I'm allowed to fantasize ...

And the Lord said unto him: 'This is the land which I swore unto Abraham, unto Isaac, and unto Jacob, saying: I will give it unto thy seed; I have caused thee to see it with thine eyes, but thou shalt not go over thither.
Deuteronomy Chapter 34 (4)

KOSHER PROHIBITIONS

My father, may he rest in peace, was a religious man. According to his Jewish forefather's tradition, the descendants of Moses, in the Torah he brought from Mount Sinai we find customs, dogmas and rules to live by today as in the days of yore.

Behind these rules is the dogma of kosher, elaborate instructions on what we are allowed to eat and what not. Hygiene rules for kitchen work and hygiene rules for the environment. Like the person commanded to rest on the seventh day, we are commanded to let the land rest in the seventh year. So it is forbidden to eat fruits and vegetables from land cultivated in the seventh year. There are also prohibitions on hybridiza-

AND IMPURE
PURE

tions of incompatible brands. This prohibition is ahead of its time, like an ancient vision of the dangers of genetic engineering

This may help to explain why I can only look at the fabulous *prosciutto* of Parma but cannot taste it, and why I avoid working on the Sabbath day. In the bakery, the Moslem holiday has passed and the Jewish holiday of Purim has arrived. A section of the bakery becomes the patisserie of another world. Tall colorful mountains of Iraqi-Jewish traditional sweets, all dripping with honey, are accumulating in the bakery. From here they will be transported to the big Mahane Yehuda market in Jerusalem. In the meantime, hundreds of customers arrive from the nearby *maabara*, a huge refugee transit camp of small aluminum sheds, in which Jews who have arrived in Israel from Arab countries and from Europe live.

They come to the bakery to taste and take in the scents of pastries and sweets with exotic traditional names: *man al-sama*, 'manna from heaven', *zingula*, *hagi-bada*, *sambosak* and 'Hamman's ears'.

But the traditional Halchic reason for them to come to buy the sweets is *Mishloh manot*— to donate portions of food. On this holiday there are two important commandments. The first good deed is to send portions of food to the poor, at least three people. The second commandment is more peculiar. This day in fact is the only one in which it is permitted to imbibe strong drinks and intoxicate oneself! Our family has a long tradition of hundreds of years of making these sweets in my birthplace in Amara, between the rivers Tigris and Euphrates in Iraq, the biblical Babel.

YOU SHALL TELL YOUR SON

On the rivers of Babylon, there they sat and cried. So go the words of the prophet and the song. They also ate fish, dreamt of Jerusalem and kept the customs of their fathers, a tradition that includes so much.

As I write these lines, the Jewish nation celebrates the Holiday of the Passover. Again the tradition of food and the tradition of rules are set against a background of issues of personal and social ecology. Starting from the 'spring cleaning' of the house and the storytelling of the *Hagada*, to be passed on to the next generations.

The word 'tradition' is all-important at the Passover Seder, when we perform traditional customs and eat traditional food: during the feast, Jews do not eat any bread or products containing barley or wheat or other grains that are fermented or leavened, from bread to beer to whisky.

The main commandment of the Passover holiday is the passing on of the tradition. The greater family gathers together to read the story of revival and emancipation of the Jewish nation. All are commanded to read the story bound in the *Hagada* revolving round the word 'to tell'. The father is commanded, 'You shall tell your son on that day, saying ...' That is how tradition is kept and passed on. As for myself, I was brought as baby from Iraq. I grew up in the Jewish tradition of the east, I deal in the traditional food of the nations of the area. At my place the tradition of my Jewish ancestors since the days of the prophets and the kings blends with the tradition of Palestine Arab cooking and the Iraqi origins of my family.

I hope that the keeping of those traditions will bring us, the nations of the area, to the same garden, where God himself plants '... every tree that is pleasing to the sight and good for food'. And that the traditional blessing for peace, Salem, will come alive with us as the prophet says:

... And they shall beat their swords into plowshares, and their spears into pruning hooks; nation shall not lift up sword against nation, neither shall they learn war any more ... Isaiah Chapter 2: 4.

PETE SEEGER, A LIVING LEGEND OF AMERICAN FOLK MUSIC FOR HIS CIVIL AND ECOLOGICAL COMMITMENT.

WHAT DO THE CLAWHAMMER BANJO AND THE SLOW FOOD PHILOSOPHY HAVE IN COMMON? THE PLEASURE OF THE LOST AND REDISCOVERED.

FLAVOR IN MUSIC

Kennet Erwin Konesni
USA, a scholar of rural communities and their music

TRADITION

I'm at the New England Folk Festival, a gathering of 10,000 folk music enthusiasts held each spring in Madison, Massachusetts. Under a blooming apple tree sit three men of different ages, each one holding a well-worn banjo. The oldest man, sporting a gray beard and tanned, wrinkled skin, is teaching a tune to the other two, one of whom can't be much older than 14. The song is upbeat but somehow mournful, played with the back of the fingernails of the right hand, which is formed into a claw and flicked in the manner of someone shaking out a dish rag. The motion strikes the strings directly, creating a rapid, repetitive plunking sound that is infectiously energetic.

This is clawhammer banjo. Also known as frailing, flailing, knockdown, rapping, or just old-time banjo, this is not the fingerpicking style of *Deliverance* fame, but an older, more archaic style brought to North America with slaves from Africa.

Fifty years ago it was on the verge of extinction, but today it can be heard at thousands of gatherings across the continent, at big festivals like this one, at small jam sessions in homes and dorm rooms. Players and listeners alike appreciate the smooth, mellow tones of the instrument when it is played in this old-time style, and they nod their heads to the hypnotic rhythmic groove of clawhammer songs.

THE PLEASURE
OF PLAYING

At the core of this comeback are values that mirror those of Slow Food. Banjo lovers honor traditions passed down from generation to generation without copyright. Like a gourmand with his wine, a banjo lover relishes the quality of a well-played tune. Players encourage fairness: many tunes are structured so that even beginners can play along, and it is standard procedure to invite newcomers into a jam session, no matter how great their ability.

And, like Slow Food, the true uniting force of old-time banjo is pleasure. It just feels so good to hear the music, and to dance or play along, that people can't help but feel that their lives are just a little bit richer because of it. Like Slow Food, this pursuit of a good life is at the heart of this Slow Folk tradition.

ECHOES OF AFRICA

The predecessor to the modern banjo, alternately called the banjar, banjil and banza, was carried to America by enslaved Africans taken to work on colonial plantations. The slaves were typically forbidden from playing drums, so they sang and played the instrument, originally made from dried and hollowed gourds, that over time evolved into the banjo as we know it today. Banjos come in many different shapes and sizes, and are generally made out of wood and metal, but a few innovative tradition-alists are making gourd banjos again, with new features and styles.

For the first 200 years in America, the banjo was played exclusively by enslaved or recently emancipated black Americans, who laid the foundation of repertoire and style that would eventually sweep America with 'banjo fever'. In the mid-1800s the instrument was rapidly picked up by Scottish, Irish and English immigrants who appreciated its haunting and evocative sounds. It spread across the country (and even to Europe) thanks to touring musical groups. Melodically driven and yet harmonically dense, the banjo was by the early 1900s a tool that helped Americans of all colors express themselves and their situations, as well as dance and sing late into the night.

REVIVAL

The five-string banjo, which in the 1880s was one of America's most popular instruments, had by the early 1950s seen its popularity decline. As the country rushed toward post-war modernization, the bright lights of electrification and industrialization threw the last rural pockets of thriving folk traditions into sharp relief. Branded as backward and unsophisticated, the tradition of playing this evocative and endearingly plunky instrument almost disappeared. Luckily, a youthful mid-20th-century folk re-

BANJO

vival—encouraged by the likes of Pete Seeger and Earl Scruggs—rediscovered the spooky pleasure of playing with friends in the kitchen and dancing through the night. Young idealists traveled into the southern Appalachian mountains to record and learn from the old-timers who were the last to remember the old songs. The music, which reflects agrarian

showed everyone that this was a tradition worth holding on to.

THE TASTE OF WHAT'S GOOD

These pioneers in the revival of clawhammer banjo have set a magnificent ball rolling. Today the banjo is being picked up by young people who are applying the values

THE PLEASURE OF LISTENING

life from its earliest days, lived on in a new, urban generation of players and aficionados. What was at first a trickle of visionaries became a stream of enthusiasts and then a torrent of music lovers. Young people from cities made their way into the countryside to document what was, at the time, a disappearing American tradition.

As they were in the process of documenting this tradition, something amazing happened. They started playing the banjo themselves. Though they began going to old-time music gatherings as observers and recorders, they soon became participants, trading songs in the way chefs trade recipes and farmers swap seeds. In so doing they convinced their friends to try out the banjo, and

of Slow Food to their music. Like I saw at the New England Folk Festival, each generation honors the old tunes and adds stylistic twists. Young people appreciate the durability of the old farmers' ballads and agrarian dance tunes, and the conviviality of playing them together. Like chefs swapping recipes or farmers swapping seeds, they understand the open-source tradition that is at the heart of the music, trading tunes and techniques at every opportunity.

Like a person biting into a perfectly ripe tomato, they understand the delicious flavor of a well-played song and its direct link to the joy and pleasure that are key elements in a good life.

Behrek ji hewa ku bête coşê
...ê-i ji dil diket xuroşê
...le aşiqane(174)
...nivan e

SCRAPBOOK

Lilia Zaouali
Tunisia, anthropologist, historian and writer
Photos Adele Obice

TRADITION

Sometimes in Turin I would have lunch at the Kirkuk Caffè. It wasn't so much the cooking that drew me there. I found the food a little too adapted to Italian tastes, being accustomed to the authentic Kurdish cuisine of the Sufi poet Seyhmus Dagtekin in Paris, and in Turin to that of the late Gibrail Giwargis Bako, a Nestorian Christian from north of Mosul in Iraq. Instead, I liked the eastern atmosphere of the place, beautiful and elegant for a change, and the owner's sincerely warm welcome.

Later I left Turin and forgot about the Kirkuk. But not long ago I received a book co-authored by Fuad Rahman, the Kirkuk Caffè's owner. The book, *Kurdistan, cucina e tradizioni del popolo curdo* (Kurdistan: Cuisine and traditions of the Kurdish people), published in 2008 by Ananke of Turin, is largely the work of Mirella Galletti, a historian of Islam; Fuad Rahman steps in only in the section dedicated to traditional Kurdish recipes.

Reading the book, I had the sensation of wandering through a maze or staring at a puzzle with many pieces missing. Right away we are informed about Fuad Rahman's identity: his father was a Muslim, originally from a Kurdish village not far from Mahabad in Iran. After

he left his family, he found a home in Kirkuk, in what is now Iraq, with a childless Armenian couple who owned a restaurant. His father fled when he was 10-years-old in 1923, the year in which the Treaty of Lausanne ratified the annexation of Kurdistan by four different countries (Syria, Iraq, Iran and Turkey). Like his adoptive parents, Fuad Rahman's father became a restaurateur, and passed on to his eleven children a culinary tradition which carries within itself as much origin as exile, two components that mark Kurdish identity and which multiply with movement, enabling a place of exile to become, in the course of time, a place of origin.

MUTTON AND RAISINS

So Fuad Rahman is an 'Iraqi Kurd,' son of an 'Iranian Kurd'. This family's story perfectly illustrates the history of Kurdish cuisine, that of a divided people and a divided land. If it is already hard to distinguish true Kurdish identity, then what is there to say about the ability to distinguish what is authentic in the culinary tradition known as Kurdish? Consider also that this tradition is known to us thanks to Turkish, Persian or Arabic terminology, rather than the three Kurdish languages.

REFLECTIONS
OF THE LAND

occasions. Despite experiencing and adopting many influences and despite cultural mutations, the Kurds have remained very attached to an ancient tradition that reveals the origins of their people, linked to a land, its products and their particular uses of those products.

DIFFERENT SOULS

Taking the land as the culinary tradition's principle reference point means placing Kurdistan at the center, but with the awareness that this center is located in the middle of other centers, aside from divisions of the country. It is a frontier land, bordering four antagonistic cultural, ethnic and political worlds: Arabic, Persian, Turkish and Russian. Plus the proximity of the Armenians and Azerbaijanis is often forgotten. Kurdistan covers an area of about 183,400 square miles, extending between the Black Sea, the Mesopotamian steppes, the eastern Taurus mountains and the Iranian plateau. With an Indo-European language and origin, the Kurds followed native beliefs derived from Zoroastrian doctrine, but today the majority are Sunni Muslims. The Shiite minorities are found mainly around Baghdad; the Alevis, other Shiites, are located in the Dersim area of Turkey, while some heterodox groups are concentrated in Kermanshah in Iran. Clearly it is easy to imagine the great diversity we must expect when tackling the subject of Kurdish cooking.

In such a complex context, the hard work of Mirella Galletti, an expert in the culture and history of Kurdistan, comes across as the task of assembling dispersed fragments, which had to be sought in all four corners of the historical land of the Kurds. She has visited many regions of Kurdistan, and she has attempted to describe Kurdish culinary traditions by taking into account the pairing of food and locality.

Is it helpful to remember that the nature of what we eat and the formation of a culinary tradition are determined, first of all, by the land? In the past, the Kurds made their living by cultivating grapevines and raising sheep; still today mutton and raisins are essential ingredients when cooking for special

THE KIRKUK KAFFE', VIA CARLO ALBERTO, TURIN.

REFLECTIONS
OF THE PAST

Is there a culinary tradition with which they identify? Certainly it exists; it is the tradition linked to rural life in the mountains or on the plateau, that of the farmers who live in the villages and the nomads who perhaps are no longer. The traditional cuisine is peasant cooking that reflects a past era. It is the figure of a woman grinding grain, a woman churning butter in a goatskin, a woman kneading dough to make bread, a woman milking goats. Women are the guardians of memory: 'In spring the sheep, in autumn the grape, in winter I am myself,' goes a Kurdish woman's proverb. So the image of a pastoral life of was perpetuated, the image of the seasonal herding of flocks and the mountains that symbolize Kurdistan. The traditional cuisine, as the Kurds themselves describe it, is the echo of an idealized popular memory, which, in my opinion, is diminishing. Seen up close, it is not such a simple cuisine. It is commonly believed that the Kurds only eat *pilaw* made from bulgur with raisins and soups of broken wheat with the addition of yogurt and meatballs with wheat. Instead, this people, supposedly closed within their own culture, possess a cuisine which bears witness to an openness to exchange with Armenian, Assyrian-Chaldean, Greco-Roman, Turkmen and Jewish traditions.

KASHA

The advent of Islam brought about the development of a Muslim cuisine, favoring exchanges with Arabs and Turks, even though it is not always possible to identify how much was borrowed and how much was handed down. *Kuliche*, a walnut-stuffed sweet said to come from Christian culture, is prepared for the important Kurdish festival of Nowruz on March 21, the Persian New Year, along with other easily transportable picnic foods (the feast is held outdoors). At the start of the 19th century, the Dominican priest, Giuseppe Campanile, who spent several years in Mosul, cites *kasha* (a porridge of previously crushed, cooked and dried wheat, bulgur) which strangely recalls the *kasha* of Russian peasants, made with buckwheat or barley, eaten during Christmas and Easter fasts, as well as Sicilian *cuccia* (wrongly or rightly attributed to the Arabs) prepared for the feast of Santa Lucia. Campanile states that the Mosul Kurds made *rescia*, none other than the Persian noodles called *reshteh*; *ch'alta*, a very elaborate dish of meat, chickpeas, raisins, dried figs, dates, onions, almonds, flour, sheep-tail fat and butter; plus *yeprak*, chard leaves stuffed with rice and mutton, said to be a Jewish specialty.

An authentically Kurdish dish? I would say *perde pilaw*, which was the subject of a debate between the descendants of the families of Prince Baba of Iraqi Kurdistan and Prince Ardelan of Iranian Kurdistan. Kurds against Kurds. In Fuad Rahman's recipe (p. 93), the mutton is replaced by chicken. Yet another innovation.

THE CAFÉ' IS RUN BY FUAD RAHMAN, CO-AUTHOR OF KURDISTAN, COOKING AND TRADITIONS OF THE KURDISH PEOPLE.

Flour House

Margarida Nogueira
Brazil, Rio de Janeiro Convivium Leader
Photos Manuel Carvalho

EDUCATION

My friend Teresa Corção, chef and owner of the O Navegador restaurant, is always interested in discovering new aspects of Brazilian cuisine. When she told me how amazed she was by the versatility of manioc and its derivatives, I was very happy but also surprised. Happy because I come from northeastern Brazil and grew up eating manioc-flour *tapiocas* and *beijus* and hearing family stories about the 'flour house', so I was pleased to find these traditions were being valued. And very surprised because I couldn't imagine that someone might not know these products which to me were so commonplace. Above all I was shocked that I had completely ignored the very real importance this root, the queen of Brazil, holds for our people.

KIDS AND DON QUIXOTES

It all started in October 2002. The background was Slow Food, with its philosophy, principles and activities. In fact the movement served as the compass that guided the birth of the project and later the Maniva institute.

A year earlier I had participated in the second edition of the Slow Food Award for the Defense of Biodiversity in Portugal as a member of the international jury. During the same period Teresa had been invited to visit the Real Companhia Velha's vineyards in the Douro region. Infected with the Slow spirit, once again I was surprised, this time to see how many incredible Don Quixotes had come from the four corners of the world to recount what they were doing to save food biodiversity. As happens to almost everyone who throws themselves headlong into Slow Food's activities, Teresa started to see the gastronomic universe in a different light, discovering a part of the world which had previously been invisible: the production of food. That was when she began not only researching manioc, but also launched the first initiative: a tapioca workshop in the Ciep Agostinho Neto public school in the south of Rio de Janeiro. The school's pupils were from three large *favelas*, Rocinha, Vidigal and Cerro-Corá, and the majority came from families originally from the northeast, families which over time had become distanced from their culture and origins. Many of the children didn't even know what tapioca was and had never heard of *beiju*, a kind of fritter made from manioc flour, which until the start of the 19th century was the 'bread' of Brazil.

This was in October, and little by little volunteers began to show up, children began to participate and the number of workshops began to grow. A tapioca competition was held at the end of every school year, a playful way of seeing how much the children had learned

and testing their culinary creativity, all under the watchful eye of a jury composed of Rio de Janeiro's best chefs.

SEU BENÉ

Subsequently we had the chance to present manioc at the 27th Annual Conference of the IACP (International Association of Culinary Professionals), held in Dallas, Texas. We shot the documentary *The Manioc Flour Professor* for the workshop, and the event was a great success. The modesty, wisdom and jollity of the main character, a small-scale *farinha d'água* (manioc flour) producer from the far-off Amazon jungle called Seu Bené, was a surprise to all. The 'professor' toured the world and took part in several film festivals, including Slow Food on Film. Seu Bené was subsequently invited to attend Terra Madre 2006 and that anthropological adventure led to the documentary *Mr Bené Goes to Italy*.

But Teresa was dreaming even bigger: more schools involved in the project, but also above all the protection of Brazil's different kinds of manioc flour. And so the Maniva institute was created to curb the loss of indigenous knowledge and to protect the rich biodiversity of the Mata Atlantica, Brazil's native coastal forest.

Around the same time the Globo network's *Canal Futura* channel offered Teresa the chance to present *Bagunça na cozinha* (chaos in the kitchen), Latin America's first taste education program. Under her guidance, children would learn about the sensory qualities and geographic origins of products, before using them to prepare 30 simple, healthy recipes.

As a result, the tapioca workshops spread to São Paulo, where they are run by students from the Semac Gastronomy School (Santo Amaro Campus), and overseen by the city's convivium. Today more than 1,700 children have taken part in the workshops in different states around Brazil.

TERESA CORÇAO AND CHILDREN IN THE MANIOC WORKSHOP.

O QUE É QUE A BAIANA TEM

In a dark corner of a Recife hotel dining room, a girl with native features is preparing tapioca for the breakfasts of the tourists and business managers, while I sip my English tea. I'm the chef and owner of a restaurant in the center of Rio de Janeiro and I've always cooked and enjoyed good food, wherever it's from. But to feed my soul, I only want Brazilian—maybe because it reminds me of my mother and aunts and the slow rhythms of childhood. The girl making the tapioca doesn't know I'm watching her. She's thinking about the customer at Table 4 who's in a rush and has asked for a mixed tapioca, with ham and cheese. I get up and walk towards her. I want to find out as much as I can about the dish. That week in Recife the restaurants were packed with people with money to spend, all here for Pernambuco state's first food festival. Professional chefs from all over the country had been invited to come and 'rediscover' local flavors. I've never trusted this kind of concept. If you don't know the foods in the first place, how can you rediscover them? Anyhow the festival organizers have sent a list of curious and completely mysterious names: *carimã* (fermented tapioca), *massa puba* (manioc fermented in water), *goma* (manioc starch). I cross the half-empty room to the dark corner where a makeshift stove has been set up. All around are emptied and filled gourds. Behind, the girl, dressed in a traditional Bahia costume, is out of breath as she mixes with ladles and spoons to conjure up a perfect tapioca, all white and soft. Interrupted by this stranger who asks her elementary questions about the product and where it's from, the nameless tapioca cook breaks off her routine work, looks up curiously and starts the lesson that continues to this day: 'Tapioca comes from starch, which is made from manioc, in the flour house...' The what house? She was my first 'manioc professor'.

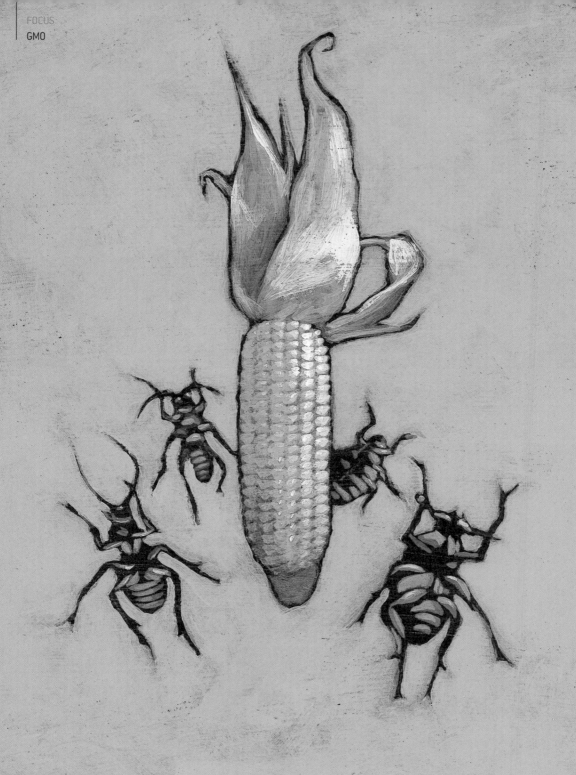

Innovative Genomes, Old Arguments

Luca Colombo
Italy, researcher at the Genetic Rights Foundation,
a biotechnology research and communication agency.

Unlike the other big technological innovations making their mark at the turn of the millennium— such as digital technology, information and communications, or medical diagnostics—plant genetic engineering has not met the expectations surrounding it. The geographical distribution of GMOs is very lopsided and mainly limited to the American continent (90 percent of global transgenic crop coverage and more than 50 percent in the United States alone); it is restricted to just four crops and two properties: tolerance to herbicides and resistance to insects.

GMO

In just a few years, GMO has become one of the most discussed, praised and condemned acronyms to appear in discussions about food, agriculture, environment, health, economics, politics and law: there are 10,100,000 Google hits for the term.

Considering that they have only been in commercial use for around 12 years, it is fair to say that transgenic crops and foods have forced themselves on public awareness like few other technological innovations, and they are certainly the most significant in the agrifood area. One might regard this as a tautological statement, given that GM crops covered 114 million hectares of land worldwide in 2007, according to the only available estimates published annually by the International Service for the Acquisition of Agri-biotech Applications (ISAAA), an organization promoting the benefits of agro-biotechnologies and supported by the major companies in the sector. There has been a steady and continuous increase in their use, without sudden rises or falls, which does not seem to reflect the campaigning and protests their introduction has provoked.

DISAPPOINTED EXPECTATIONS

However, unlike the other big technological innovations making their mark at the turn of the millennium—such as digital technology, information and communications, or medical diagnostics—plant genetic engineering has not met the expectations and predictions surrounding it. The geographical distribution of GMOs is very lopsided and mainly limited to the American continent (90 percent of global transgenic crop coverage and more than 50 percent in the United States alone); it is restricted in agricultural and botanical terms to just four crops (soy, corn, cotton and rapeseed); it is technologically limited to only two properties targeted by agronomic objectives: principally tolerance to herbicides, and resistance to insects. Given all the talk about innovation and the modernization of agricultural activity, one could in fact say there has been *technological stagnation*, if it is true that today the supply of

transgenic seeds is the same as when they were commercially introduced in the mid-1990s.

There are two interrelated explanations for this. On the one hand, it is necessary to pay for the significant research and development costs associated with bringing a transgenic variety to the market (estimated in tens of millions of dollars), which forces companies to focus on genetic modifications likely to be accepted by a large enough number of farmers that can afford the cost. On the other hand, consumers have shown a largely hostile attitude towards transgenic food and this has limited the range of GMOs to a few commodities mainly intended for animal feed or textile use. So for this reason products mainly intended for direct human consumption, such as genetically-modified wheat, rice, tomatoes, potatoes or sugar, though prepared for the market, have had to be rapidly reconsidered due to a lack of commercial prospects. Similar optimistic predictions, though the products were never commercially available, were made for plants tolerating drought or salinity, those with increased resistance to pathogens or providing more nutrients.

Though gene transfer science has achieved significant technological advances, transgenic agriculture is an exact continuation of the high-productivity approach that preceded it and partly inspired its development. It is highly dependent on production factors external to the farm and agro-ecological system; it simplifies cultivation, requiring minimal inputs of labor and little human supervision of the cultivation system; it requires significant amounts of capital (and if there is insufficient liquidity, debts) to support technological investments; agricultural production is standardized and geared to the subsequent phase of industrial processing; the production chain is long—and very long in terms of geographical distances, added value generated, numbers and varieties of different parties involved. The basic criteria of transgenic agriculture are no different to those used by industrialized agriculture in recent decades and, it should be remembered, they have been seriously challenged for their ecological and health impacts, as well as various serious scandals.

STATELESS AND ANONYMOUS

However, while maintaining many aspects of continuity with the previous approach, agro-biotechnology brings some new features which increase concerns about the prospects for food and the right to food. Contract farming (the mechanism which ties a farmer to the agribusiness company with regard to quantity, time and quality of supplies) has been established to meet the requirements of large retail chains. It is reinforced by transgenic agriculture as a result of contractual rules governing the use of seeds—a natural complement to the right to patent transgenic plants which has been introduced into the laws of many countries and which it is intended to control at international level through the World Trade Organization.

We find a paradoxical situation: transgenic seeds can be exclusively owned through the patent and contracts stipulating the terms of cultivation, they are fully described and identified; yet the food produced is stateless and without origin in the eyes of consumers. GMOs in fact are a maximum expression of anonymous food. They are anonymous in countries where the public is not allowed labeling showing the presence or use of transgenic ingredients: this is the case in the main countries growing GMOs such as the USA, Canada or Argentina. They are anonymous in Europe, where genetically modified crops are used for livestock without disclosure, also due to the fact that food obtained from animals fed with GMOs are not subject to labeling requirements. They are anonymous wherever possible because invisibility is crucial where the market does not accept them.

INTERNAL RESISTANCE

The inherent invisibility of GMOs has been decisively challenged by the protest action around the world focusing attention on these new foods and making public opinion aware, critical and involved. GMOs have in fact had the merit of reviving interest in food—how and by whom it has been grown, processed and sold—as well as reopening debate on the role of science and research in 21st-century society, even within the world of science itself.

The fact that there is widespread attention within society to GMOs is undoubtedly one of the significant features of the transgenic crops issue and a participative food democracy, but protests were not the only obstacle to the expansion of transgenic agriculture. Another threat to its deployment is the way in which the technology was conceived, plus the commercial excitement surrounding it. The large-scale adoption of GM seeds in countries where the transgenic model is accepted is paradoxically also one of the main limitations on their continued expansion. Ever more frequently, scientific literature reports the development of resistance by target organisms (butterfly larvae which develop resistance to the Bt toxin expressed by the modified plant are an example) and of toxic or lethal effects on non-target organisms (such as other harmless insects). Similar examples can be cited of wild herbs which have become tolerant to herbicides applied on GM crops: this is a serious worry for farmers and a problem for the agroecosystem. Attempts are then sometimes made to resolve these phenomena by inserting new transgenic variants into the genome of the modified plants, prompting renewed technological intervention reminiscent of the spiral of poisons used in chemical agriculture in the 1970s and 1980s.

But you can't resolve a problem with the same head as the one that created it, as Einstein remarked. Somebody should tell those people—for example in the Cartagena Biosafety Protocol negotiations—who think that the problems of gene flow with transgenic crops and their ecological invasion can be resolved with technologies such as the Terminator gene (a technology restricting genetic use, which produces sterile plants in the second generation, obliging farmers to buy seeds each season). Somebody should also tell those people in the economy and the media taking advantage of the recent food crisis to promote GMOs, which are neither the cause nor the solution to the problem.

At stake is the future of food, the future of growers and the future of those who have to eat. In other words all of us.

South American Harvest

Miguel A. Altieri
Chile, lecturer in agroecology,
University of California, Berkeley

Biotech companies claim that herbicides should not pose negative effects on humans or the environment. in practice, however, the large-scale planting of GM crops encourages aerial application of herbicides and only 1.% of what is sprayed reaches the crop and the rest ends up in the soil and water bodies.

GMO

In 2007, GM crops reached 114.3 million hectares worldwide. Of the 23 countries which grow GM crops, Argentina and Brazil stand out in South America, though transgenic crops are also expanding in Bolivia and Paraguay, for example. The biotech industry claims that GM crops have met the expectations of millions of farmers in developing countries, delivering benefits to consumers and society through more affordable food that require less pesticide and hence leads to a more sustainable environment. What corporations fail to mention is that 70 percent of GM crops grown are Roundup Ready soybean, a crop tolerant to Monsanto's herbicide glyphosate, mainly grown by large-scale farmers for biodiesel and for export as animal feed to China and Europe. The impacts of soybean expansion in South America go beyond the typical effects of monocultures heavily sprayed with herbicides, but include deforestation, soil fertility mining, food insecurity and the expulsion of small farmers, thus augmenting rural conflicts.

DEFORESTATION AND THE FATE OF FARMERS

The expansion of soybean is accompanied by massive transportation infrastructure projects that lead to the destruction of natural habitats over wide areas, well beyond the deforestation directly caused by soybean cultivation. In Brazil, soybean profits justified the improvement or construction of industrial waterways, railway lines and an extensive network of roads. These in turn have attracted logging, mining, ranching and other practices with severe impacts on biodiversity. The Rosario region on the Parana river in Argentina has become the largest soy agro-industrial processing area in the world, with all the environmental impacts that such infrastructure entails. Soybean today occupies the largest area of any crop in Brazil (14.5 million hectares). In Argentina about 16 million hectares are devoted to soybean and the total production is more than 40 million tones. In Paraguay soybeans occupy more than 25 percent of all agricultural land. Soy cultivation has already resulted in the deforestation of 21 million hectares of forests in Brazil, 14 million hectares in Argentina, two million hectares in Paraguay and 600,000 hectares in Bolivia. In response to global market pressure for biofuels, Brazil alone will likely clear an additional 60 million hectares of land in the near future to grow more soybean for biodiesel and sugar cane for ethanol.

Soybean expansion also leads to extreme land and income concentration. In Brazil, soybean cultivation displaces 11 agricultural workers for every one who finds employment in the sector. Yearly, millions of people are displaced by soybean production and these landless people move to the Amazon and other regions where they clear pristine forests. In Argentina, the situation is quite dramatic as 60,000 farms went out of business, while the area of GM soybean almost tripled. In one decade, soybean area increased 126 percent at the expense of dairy, maize, wheat and fruit production. For the country, this means more imports of basic foods, hence loss of food sovereignty, and for poor small farmers and consumers, only increased food prices and more hunger.

VICIOUS CIRCLE

As the soybean area rapidly expands, so does glyphosate use. In southern Brazil, for every kilogram of non-glyphosate herbicide reduced during the period of expansion of GM soybean, the use of glyphosate increased by 7.5 kilograms. In Argentina, Roundup applications reached the equivalent of an estimated 160 million liters in the 2004 growing season. Herbicide usage is expected to increase as weeds start developing resistance to Roundup. A recent study by Brazilian researchers found 13 weed species that have developed resistance to glyphosate. In Argentina, resistant biotypes of Johnsongrass, *Verbena* sp. and *Ipomoea* sp. and other weeds are also emerging, creating a typical treadmill in which Glyphosate generates weeds that are harder to control, which in turn require increased amounts of other herbicides such as 2,4-D. Instead of reducing the need for agrochemicals—as proponents once claimed—GM technology has increased their use.

Biotech companies claim that herbicides should not pose negative effects on humans or the environment. In practice, however, the large-scale planting of GM crops encourages aerial application of herbicides and only 1 percent of what is sprayed reaches the crop and the rest ends up in the soil and water bodies[1]. The companies contend that glyphosate degrade rapidly in the soil, do not accumulate in ground water, have no effects on non-target organisms, leave no residue in foods and water or soil. Yet glyphosate has been reported to be toxic to some non-target species in the soil—both to beneficial predators such as spiders, mites and carabid and coccinellid beetles, and to detritivores such as earthworms, including mycorrizae and other microfauna, as well as to aquatic organisms, including microbial communities, frogs and fish.

BIOLOGICAL ALTERATIONS

Research has shown that glyphosate seems to act in a similar fashion to antibiotics, altering soil biology in yet unknown ways and causing effects such as: reduction of the ability of soybeans, clover and other legumes to fix nitrogen; the rendering of bean plants more vulnerable to disease. During the first year of glyphosate application on RR soya, a severe sudden death syndrome epidemic occurred (infection by the fungus *Fusarium solani)*in several RR cultivars; reduction of the growth of beneficial soil-dwelling mycorrhizal fungi, which are a key to helping plants extract phosphorous from the soil; changes to the microbial community in the inter-row soil in vineyards (caused by herbicide use in a 2.5 year study in Australia). Soil from plots that had been repeatedly treated with herbicide contained lower populations of cellulolytic bacteria, *Pseudomonas* spp. and fungi.

All above reported effects can alter nutrient cycling and other important processes in the soil thus reducing plant growth and health. In a study using outdoor tanks, researchers found that even when applied at concentrations that are just one third of the maximum concentrations expected in nature, glyphosate killed 98 percent of all tadpoles within three weeks and 79 percent of all frogs within one day[2]. In Argentina researchers using artificial earthen mesocosms found that applications of Roundup decreased micro and nanophytoplancton in treated mesocosms.

Researchers have also showed that the reduction of weed biomass, flowering and seeding parts under herbicide resistant crop management causes changes in insect resource availability with knock-on effects resulting in abundance reduction of several beetles, butterflies and bees. Counts of predacious carabid beetles that feed on weed seeds were smaller in transgenic crop fields. The number of invertebrates that are food for mammals, birds and other invertebrates were also found to be generally lower in herbicide resistant crop fields. The absence of flowering weeds in transgenic fields can have serious consequences for pollinators but also for pests' natural enemies, which require pollen and nectar for survival, and which in turn can lead to enhanced insect pest problems.

TENSIONS

The expansion of soybean monoculture threatens the ecological integrity and food sovereignty of countries as well as the rights of indigenous and rural communities. This industrial agricultural model violates economic, social, cultural and environmental rights and, as it expands, its destructive methods of operation degrade the environment through deforestation, soil erosion, contamination of water bodies and push farmers out of their lands, resulting in rural migration and further impoverishment of rural populations. The soy agroindustry is actually expanding and becoming stronger through the growing markets for processed foods, industrial livestock and the production of biodiesel demanded by the North. Rural social movements such as Via Campesina and MST reject corporate attempts to continual expansion of GM soy monoculture. Farmers' mobilizations have led to destruction of soybean fields and occupations of corporate facilities. For example, Syngenta Seeds' experimental research center was taken over by MST in Parana last March 2006, after they discovered that the company was illegally growing GM soybeans within the boundary zone of the Iguaçu National Park. The expansion of agricultural biotechnology into South America is exacerbating agrarian conflicts and historic tensions over land. More mobilizations of rural movements can be expected, as the grassroots movement opposing the advance of biofuel agribusiness and GM technology grows. Industrial farming threatens biodiversity and native seed varieties, violating the rights of consumers and small farmers by contaminating conventional and organic crops. If consumers in the North of the world want to continue enjoying their fair trade coffee and bananas, as well as the 'good, clean and fair food' from the South, they had better find ways to directly support these grassroots mobilizations, otherwise small farmers and the food they grow, so precious to northern consumers, are at danger of GM pollution and possible extinction.

1. Pimentel, D and H. Lehman, *The Pesticide Question*, Chapman and Hall, New York 1993.

2. Relyea, R.A., 'The Impact of Insecticides and Herbicides on the Biodiversity and Productivity of Aquatic Communities', *Ecological Applications* 15 2005, pp. 618-627.

GREEN ¿

The World's Breadbasket

Maria Teresa Morresi
Argentina, a journalist with *La Nación*, specialized in ecology, organic agriculture, social welfare and NGOs

The boom in biofuels opens new prospects. The government and companies are pushing for them to be adopted, and this means more GMOs both for production of animal feed and for biofuels, which are derived from corn and soy in particular.

GMO

'Argentina is the second biggest producer of GMOs in the world. Its 19,846,000 hectares dedicated to genetically-modified agricultural products account for 17 percent of the global total. In first place is the United States and Brazil is third, with a number of other countries enthusiastically adopting these products, while others, where restrictions applied, are abandoning them. In 2007 the number of GMO producers worldwide reached 2 million,' observes Dina Foguelman, ecologist and member of MAPO, *Movimiento Argentino para la Producción Orgánica* (Argentine Movement for Organic Production, www.mapo.org.ar).

LEGUMES

The exponential development of transgenic products began ten years ago with soy. This crop now covers 16.6 million hectares and is taking over both on soils considered among the most fertile in the world—such as the damp pampas—and on land in desert areas rejected by agriculture due to low fertility. The data are disturbing: GM crops grow on 63 percent of the 30 million hectares cultivated with different varieties of cereals and legumes, with a definite prevalence of soybean. 'The technological package involves using Rg soybean, the herbicide glyphosate and direct sowing,' explains Walter Pengue, director of the Master of Ecological Economics at the Faculty of Architecture in Buenos Aires and coordinator of the interdisciplinary academic group GEPAMA (*Grupo de Ecología del Paisaje y Medio Ambiente*, www.gepama.com.ar): 'Mixed cultivation is eliminated,' continues Pengue. 'This transforms the pampas and elsewhere into a monoculture area. The new soybean crop is the basis for a model of intensive production which creates a sales value of 11 billion dollars.'

The technological change is focused on legume crops and ignores cereals. There has been a significant displacement of livestock farming towards marginal areas (the Chaco region in the north of the country, for example) or it is concentrated in small areas of the pampas specifically dedicated to fattening animals. In ten years the production of cereals and legumes has tripled, increasing from 30 million to more than 100 million tons of product in the last year, without there being a significant reduction in livestock farming. 'This process,' comments the agronomist, 'is supported by a very favorable international market which, as in the case of China, is increasing demand and the variable but rising prices boost the value of raw material production.'

PAST SPLENDORS

Thanks to soy the country is perhaps returning to being the 'breadbasket of the world', to the great relief of producers who manage to combine efficiency and profits. Legume crops are also a shot in the arm for the shaky Argentine economy, which according to analysts, is benefiting greatly from exports. Soy has been so extensively adopted that it is hard to find a plot of land or rural roadside strip that doesn't grow it.

At the same time natural forests—whether degraded by exploitation or in healthy state—are becoming a piece of natural heritage at risk of extinction. This emergency has prompted environmental organizations to conduct a long battle for the introduction of a law protecting the forest heritage. With support from over $1^{1}/_{2}$ million citizens, law n. 26331 *Presupuestos Mínimos de Protección Ambiental de los Bosques Nativos* (Minimum Requirements for the Environmental Protection of Natural Forests, of December 19, 2007) was issued, stipulating a moratorium on further felling until each province has implemented its own territorial regulations. The advance of land converted to growing crops has not respected the rich plant and animal resources that created various ecosystems.

CEREALS BANNED

In many areas the habitat has been seriously disrupted to make space for the enticing legumes, which promise excellent yields and attractive markets; cereal crops have been abandoned: wheat and corn or seedlings such as sunflower have been reduced to 4 million hectares and 2.6 million respectively. It should also be remembered that in many cases, for example corn and sunflower, not only GM seeds are involved.

'The owners of degraded fields,' says Foguelman, 'can recover productivity if they plant soybean, since the legume will grow practically anywhere. They also benefit from increased rainfall due to climate change. So a lot of land has gained value'. Average producers who cannot afford the cost of agricultural methods based on technology, have begun to sell their plots of land. We are returning to a situation of 'seed pools', where producers are transformed into rentiers on their own land, and trusts are formed. In this invasion of soy it is interesting to note that Gustavo Grobocopatel, a businessman of the Los Grobos group, now owns 105,000 hectares of completely cultivated land. 'Transgenic products,' states ecologist Dina Foguelman, 'seem to be associated with direct sowing. Like every technology, this one has its pros and cons. If we look at the benefits, there is a reduction in the use of machinery and energy and, shortly afterwards, significant protection of the organic matter in the soil and a reduction of soil erosion. Furthermore it is said that in 10 years the system will have generated a million jobs. On the other hand, we don't know the long-term advantages and as the land is not worked, chemical products are required to control infestations, with serious adverse effects on biodiversity'.

GM IMPACT

GMOs jeopardize organic farming, so specific policies should be implemented to address this risk (in Argentina 3,000,000 hectares of land are certified organic). Foguelman explains that, 'GM technology is rejected by organic producers and prohibited through specific regulations. Where GMOs are used, there must be buffer areas between fields measuring 250 meters for corn and 800 for cotton. Exact figures have not been defined for soy, where contamination during transport is a problematic issue'.

Not many studies have been carried out in Argentina regarding the impact of transgenic organisms on health and soils. Experts say that there is not much money for research and negative data tends to be played down. 'Our country,' says Foguelman, 'is a guinea pig. Here the *Administración Nacional de Medicamentos, Alimentos y Tecnología Médica* (ANMAT), the National Agency for Drugs, Food and Medical Devices, does not require labeling, and in any case every common food product contains some GMOs. Fortunately the *Instituto Nacional de Tecnología Agropecuaria* (INTA), the National Institute for Agricultural and Livestock Technologies, has begun to provide more critical responses and comments. A technology is not a solution; the solution must be political.'

RETENCIONES

The boom in biofuels opens new prospects. The government and companies are pushing for them to be adopted, and this means more GMOs both for production of animal feed and for biofuels, which are derived from corn (bioethanol) and soy (biodiesel) in particular. 'The state "lives off" exported natural resources through the *retenciones* [withholding taxes],' comments Pengue. 'The tax on soy granules has increased from 27.5 to 35 percent since November 2007; for oil the increase is from 24 to 32 percent; for wheat from 20 to 28 percent; for corn from 20 to 25 percent, for sunflower from 23.5 to 32 percent. The companies pay, seeing that they can then fuel the vicious circle that allows them to influence the production policies in the country. In addition they control the scientific and technological system, the legislative and even the judicial system.'

According to Pengue, for every three ships carrying grain and legumes from Argentina, one is for the state in the form of withholding taxes or export duties. 'In the 2007 season,' adds Pengue, 'the amount reached 4,680 million dollars. Using these figures for the record production expected for the 2007-2008 season (97.7 million tons of cereals; 9.2 of oil and 34 of flour) and taking account of rising prices (they have increased 22 percent in one year), tax revenue can be forecast at 7,200 million dollars'. And this is not all. There is an increase in the use of chemical products, both herbicides, such as 2,4-D, paraquat, and glyphosate (whose consumption has risen from 1 million liters to over 180 million) and insecticides used for the 'protective' treatment of seeds.

EFFICIENCY

It is difficult for this process to be stopped. Global demand for soy from Europe, China and India, and new demand for biofuels, is driving a search for new cultivable land. But Argentina has to address the still open question of territorial regulations, which is a strategic problem. Furthermore, there are spreading infestations of immune and resistant weeds, such as Aleppo grass (*Sorghum halepense*). The state has done very little, though it is responsible for dealing with the situation. While they admit the existence of the problem, companies are slow to give relevant information to the state. According to Pengue, the environmental protection system is inadequate, partial and not managed transparently. It is essential to introduce improvements and intervene at local level, with independent and responsible bodies carrying out research work to systematically determine the current situation. Clive James, founder of the International Service for the Acquisition of Agri-Biotech Applications (ISAAA), takes a pragmatic view: 'In Argentina, where it is not possible to expand cultivable land, unlike the situation in Brazil, the objective must be to increase productivity to the maximum. In the short term it is important to increase the efficiency of growing GM crops. The biofuel debate is an issue to be addressed in the longer term'.

Thus Spoke Percy

Pamela Cuthbert
Canada, food journalist for *The Economist*
and *The Globe and Mail*

Last spring, after a decade-long, David-and-Goliath battle that pitted Canadian Prairie canola farmer Percy Schmeiser against multinational seed giant Monsanto, the 77-year-old folk hero won a $660 cheque from the multinational company. The money was hardly the point. The farmer won a moral victory that might offer hope for his peers around the world who continue to face similar struggles: he won the right to freedom of speech.

GMO

The payment was nothing more than a drop in the bucket, but its impact could prove to have a lasting and significant ripple effect. Last spring, after a decade-long, David-and-Goliath battle that pitted Canadian Prairie canola farmer Percy Schmeiser against multinational seed giant Monsanto, the 77-year-old folk hero won a $660 cheque from the multinational company. The money was hardly the point. The farmer won a moral victory that might offer hope for his peers around the world who continue to face similar struggles: he won the right to freedom of speech.

In a landmark case, Mr. Schmeiser tried and failed to win a different kind of victory: the right to seed. Beginning in 1997 and ending in 2004, with a Supreme Court of Canada ruling in Monsanto's favour, the farmer was sued for violating the agrichemical company patent on genetically modified (GM) canola seeds, called Round-up Ready, and engineered to resist Monsanto-brand herbicide. The court stated that plant genes and modified cells can be patented. Mr. Schmeiser had always maintained his farm had, in fact, been contaminated with GM seed that had blown onto his canola fields.

OIL!

Canola, generally consumed as an oil or fat in processed products such as margarine, was developed through plant breeding techniques in the 1970s in Canada—the name refers to 'Canada oil'. A strain of rapeseed suitable for intensive farming and related to mustard, it is processed into a cooking and table oil with the naturally bold flavor removed, in part, through heat treatment. Inexpensive to produce and purchase, it has low levels of saturated fat and is suitable for high-temperature cooking in deep fryers and for other supply fast-food needs. Little wonder it became the country's major oilseed crop, especially after the introduction in 1995 of GM canola. Today, more than 80 percent of canola production in Canada is GM.

Because the plant cross-pollinates, the dominance of GM seed has pushed producers such as Alberta's Highland Crossing farmer Tony Marshall out of the field—literally. Mr. Marshall produces a cold-pressed, non-GM canola oil that embraces the plant's aromatic roots. He used to grow his own seed. But given the issues of cross-contamination, he could no longer guarantee his own canola crops as non-GM and has since sought out farmers in remote locales. He works with farmers up north, in Peace River country, and to be certain he sends out random samples for DNA testing.

MINOR VICTORIES

On their long road to victory, the Schmeisers also lost their status as canola growers, along with many years of research spent developing varieties suited to their environment. The seeds were contaminated with the Roundup Ready gene. It's an all too common story.

The Organic Agriculture Protection Fund Committee, a group of Prairie certified organic farmers, including the seed-saving activist and protector/grower of Canada's first Ark product Red Fife wheat, Marc Loiselle, has been fighting for more than six years to get compensation for losses due to contamination of certified organic crops and fields by GM canola owned by Monsanto Canada and Bayer Crop Science. The fact that the introduction of GM wheat was stopped, and that no new GM crops have been introduced into Canadian agriculture since the committee began lobbying for legal action are two small victories—for now. But in December of last year, they were once again turned down, this time by the Supreme Court of Canada. Six months earlier, there was a pull in the opposite direction – a positive one for farmers—south of the border. The Public Patent Foundation (PUBPAT) announced that the US Patent and Trademark Office rejected four key Monsanto patents relating to GM crops that are at the heart of a struggle very reminiscent of the Schmeiser case, with the biotech firm filing patent infringement lawsuits against American farmers for the 'crime' of saving seed from one year's crop to replant the following year.

MONSANTO PAYS

In 2005, a new crop of the same offending Monsanto canola sprouted on the Schmeisers' farm, but this time the farmer and his wife, Louise, took care of pulling out the plants and sent Monsanto the bill. The tally: $660. What came next was tantamount to a gag order offered in exchange for payment, but the Schmeisers stood firm. Monsanto has a longstanding reputation for getting its way, but the Schmeisers would tough it out, as they did many years ago when the company offered to withdraw the original lawsuit if the couple agreed to buy their seed from Monsanto and pay the biotech firm a fee. Finally, in the winter of 2008, the Schmeisers won the right to disclose the terms of their settlement with Monsanto. At the same time, there was news of several Canadian farmers who signed Monsanto's release form —16 alone in 2007—who are forbidden to reveal the terms of their agreements. It had taken the Schmeisers an additional two-and-a-half years and more legal fees, but when they received their cheque for $660 in the small-claims court case, it came with full disclosure.

TONS OF OIL

In 2007, the Schmeisers were honoured with the Right Livelihood Award (the alternative Nobel Prize) for their tireless campaigning, which continued after Monsanto successful lawsuit against them, sending a message around the world warning farmers they no longer had the right to save seed. The jurors applauded the couple 'for their courage in defending biodiversity and farmers' rights, and challenging the environmental and moral perversity of current interpretations of patent laws'.

Meanwhile, GM Canola continues to spread around world. In 2008, in spite of major protests, Monsanto and Bayer finally won the legal right to have GM canola planted in much of Australia. With the push to reduce if not eliminate transfats from restaurant chains, the demand for canola oil is on the rise. As the world's major canola-oil producer, Canada has plans for a 15-million-tonne target by 2015—an increase of 65 percent—that will mean planting an extra 4 million acres of the crop, mainly displacing the country's largest crop, wheat. As for the open-book ruling, Mr. Schmeiser commented in a newspaper interview, it's 'a great victory for farmers all over the world ... an opportunity to have some recourse on a corporation when they are contaminated'.

The figures don't add up

Vandana Shiva
India, scientist and economist, founder of the Research
Foundation for Science, Technology and Ecology, which led to
the creation of Navdanya, a non-governmental organization
that promotes biodiversity conservation, especially the
process of seed saving

it is simply not true that Bt cotton has
spelt benefits for Indian farmers, and
the suicides in Bt cotton areas are the
strongest proof of the fact.

GMO

In 2007, 1,095 farmers committed suicide—one every eight hours—in the Vidharbha region of the Indian state of Maharashtra. Vidharbha has emerged as an epicentre of farmers' suicides over the last decade. It is also the region in which Monsanto sells most of its genetically-engineered Bt cotton (grown with the insect-resistant bacterium *B. thuringiensis*). In 2002, the first year Bt was approved for commercial planting, there was no such cotton in Maharashtra. By 2006, land allotted for its cultivation in the state had reached 435,000 acres.

'More Bt=more suicides' is a stark correlation, yet Vidharbha Jan Andolan, a farmers' advocacy group, has mapped suicides and Bt sales in Vidharbha, district by district, and has come up with the conclusion that districts with the highest Bt cultivation also have the highest suicide rates. Farmers' suicides area direct result of indebtedness, and even the Indian Government has been forced to recognize the fact by announcing a Rs. 60,000 crore loan waiver.

HUMAN COSTS

We speak of 'Seeds of Suicide' because, at the centre of this agrarian crisis, is Bt cotton:

i) because its seeds are costly. Conventional cotton seeds cost Rs. 200/kg, Bt cotton seeds cost Rs. 3,600/kg. The Andhra Pradesh government was even forced to take Monsanto to the MRTP Court, India's antitrust body, because of its charging exorbitant prices. Since farmers cannot afford to pay for the seeds, they accept credit from seed agents and are subsequently trapped in debt. Not that the problem is unique to India. Nearly a decade ago, during a trip to the US, I asked farmers growing Monsanto's Round Up Resistant Corn why they bought it. The farmers replied that they had no option. 'The corporations hold a noose round our necks. We have to buy whatever they sell.'

ii) because Bt cotton seeds are non-renewable. Farmers have to buy them every year, thus increasing their costs.

iii) because, while Bt cotton is sold as a pest-resistant seed, it is in fact only resistant to the American bollworm—or at least as long as it takes the bollworm to develop resistance to it.

Bt cotton is, instead, vulnerable to many other pests such as aphids and jassids, meaning that farmers have to continue to spray pesticides, thus increasing cultivation costs. iv) because Bt genes have been introduced into hybrids and hybrids need irrigation. In rainfed regions, farmers must either borrow more money for tube wells or face crop failure in the event of erratic rainfall.

The biotechnology industry is fabricating data to present Bt. cotton as a miracle. The hybrid seeds are advertised and promoted in the most unethical ways. Companies can sell what they want on what terms they want, with no one to keep a check. Among other things, globalization has removed any regulation on the seed sector. Yes, globalization is the deregulation of commerce. Behind the hype are the biotech industry group International Service for the Acquisition of Agri-Biotech Applications (ISAA) and its chairman Clive James. But the publicity is clearly failing to keep up its promises. Vidharbha's farmers are *not* becoming millionaires by growing Bt cotton. The claim of industry-sponsored studies like those carried out by organizations such as IMRB International and Assocham that Bt cotton has increased productivity and farmers' incomes is false. The industry has claimed four times more reduction in pesticide use, 12 times more yield and 100 times more profit than our field studies suggest.

We have found that Bt cotton farmers were incurring average losses of up to Rs. 6400/acre. A report released by Youth for Voluntary Action in association with Greenpeace India and Centre for Sustainable Agriculture shows that farmers who used non-Bt cotton in the 2005 kharif season had net incomes almost 62 percent higher than those who opted for Bt cotton. This was because, despite a marginally higher yield, the cost of cultivation for Bt cotton was also over 33 percent higher.

SPEND AND YIELD

Farmers who cultivate Bt cotton do so in the hope that it will reduce their spending on pesticide sprays and substantially improve their yields. But they ultimately spend 15 percent of the total cost of cultivation on the seed, whereas non-Bt farmers spend only 5 percent. Non Bt cotton farmers, moreover, show an average yield of 276 kg/ha against the Bt cotton farmers' 180 kg/ha. So, despite spending 3.5 times more on pesticide-resistant seed, a Bt farmer achieves only a 4 percent reduction in pesticide costs, and ends up with a 35 percent loss on final yield.

It is simply not true that Bt cotton has spelt benefits for Indian farmers, and the suicides in Bt cotton areas are the strongest proof of the fact.

The first myth about GM crops is that they will reduce hunger, but neither GM cotton nor GM maize go to feed people. GM maize, once used as cattle fodder in factory farms, is now being increasingly diverted to the production of biofuels.

ILLEGAL EMBRACES

A second myth is that increased cotton production and exports in India are linked to Bt cotton productivity. Clive James has stated that, 'The rapid strides that India has made in cotton production since the country embraced Bt Cotton and the fact that it has overtaken the U.S speak volumes about the technology'. But India did not 'embrace' Bt Cotton: Bt. Cotton was thrust upon Indian farmers—in the first instance illegally.

The Research Foundation for Science, Technology and Ecology initially challenged the import and field trials of Bt cotton insofar as they violated the 'Rules for the Manufacture, Use, Import, Export and Storage of Hazardous Microorganisms, Genetically Engineered Organisms or Cells 1989', framed under the Environment Protection Act 1986. whereby imports and field trials require approval from the Genetic Engineering Approval Committee. Yet Monsanto and Mahyco had no such approval. Subsequently, the first three varieties of Bt cotton approved in 2002 in southern states were rejected for planting in 2005 due to high levels of crop failure.

LIVES IN PIECES

The increase in cotton acreage is a result of the Indian government's turning its back on food grains and promoting cash crops. Between 1991 and 2001, more than eight million acres of food growing land was diverted to export crops. Since 2001 the loss of food growing land has further increased. When quantitative restrictions were removed in 2001, cotton imports shot up as cheap subsidized cotton from the US was dumped on Indian markets. They have since dropped as a result of Brazil's initiating a case against U.S on cotton subsidies. In the meantime, the $4 billion subsidy that went to 20,000 farmers in the US had destroyed the lives and incomes of millions of farmers in Africa and India.

Today India is exporting large quantities of cotton, partly as a result of the trade liberalization regime that has led to destruction of its cotton textile industry. It is now exporting cotton to China and importing textiles and clothing from China. In short, cotton production is growing as is the area of land allotted to Bt cotton cultivation. This is all a result of policies that are working against food sovereignty, and the fact that corporate monopolies have destroyed the seed supply of farmers.

ASHA KE BEEJ

That is why we, members of the Navdanya rural development movment, have started the 'Asha ke Beej' (Seeds of Hope) campaign, to offer farmers alternatives to Bt cotton in the 'suicide belt' of Vidharbha. Besides providing guidance and help to the farmers for the revival of agriculture, we distribute indigenous seed varieties among them and encourage them to move to organic and sustainable agriculture.

Navdanya has now distributed seeds to more than 10,000 farmers and widows of suicide victims. Our commitment to the Vidharbha region is to create fair trade for its organic produce, including cotton, and to help its farmers elude the vicious circle of the debt trap in agriculture, which is leading to farmers' suicides.

So far the enthusiasm has been amazing. Our ultimate aim is to create GMO-free, patent-free, debt-free and suicide-free villages, to bring back the seeds of food crops and non-Bt cotton, promoting low-cost, high-output ecological farming. Organic cotton and food sovereignty are India's future. Not Bt cotton.

NeW!
FReSH!
LeThAL!

The Debate
in Australia

Richard Cornish
Australia, food writer

A shopper could buy a tub of margarine made entirely from GM canola without a single word about genetic modification appearing anywhere on the packaging. Australian shoppers buy imported soft drinks made with modified corn syrup from GM corn, but as the GM corn syrup is 'highly refined', the drink does not carry GM on its labelling. Foods made from animal products are not covered by the standard unless the animal itself is genetically modified.

GMO

Read the papers and you'd think that 2008 was the year Australia went GM with the first commercial plantings of GM canola. The true story, however, is that Australians have been eating foods made from GM-derived products for over a decade. This would come as quite a shock to most Australians.

At the beginning of the year two state governments, Victoria, then New South Wales, lifted bans on growing commercial GM crops. The first commercial GM canola seeds were then sown in the southern autumn. The government in Queensland has always supported GM and the state has extensive plantings of GM cotton. Bans on planting commercial GM crops have been retained in South Australia, Tasmania and Western Australia. Genetically modified foods have been on Australian shop shelves since the 1990s. Imported manufactured foods using GM soy products and GM corn products such as canned meats and soft drinks were at the time imported under existing laws. In 1999 a specific food standard, A -18, came into effect, banning the sale of GM food unless certain conditions were met. This was rolled over into Food Standards Australia New Zealand (FSANZ) Standard 1.5.2 that strictly prohibited the sale of GM foods unless they are one of the 33 approved and listed GM foods, including corn, cotton seed, soy, potato, canola or sugar beet. Labelling of all GM foods came into force in 2001, so foods containing GM ingredients, such as 'Soy Flour. Genetically Modified', must be labelled.

TRICKS OF THE TRADE

There is, however, what many have called a loophole in this standard. Foods made with genetically modified ingredients that have been 'highly refined', as defined by the standard, such as GM cotton seed oil, GM canola oil and GM corn syrup, do not need to be labelled as GM. This was a decision made by FSANZ under the Liberal (centre-right) government at the time, which had a pro GM agenda.

The legacy of this loophole is confusion and uncertainty at the supermarket checkout. A shopper could buy a tub of margarine made entirely from GM canola without a single word about genetic modification appearing anywhere on the packaging. Australian shoppers buy imported soft drinks made with modified corn syrup from GM corn, but as the GM corn syrup is 'highly refined', the drink does not carry GM on its labelling. Foods made from animal products are not covered by the standard unless the animal itself is genetically modified. So milk from a cow that is fed GM cotton seed trash or one of the glyphosate tolerant lucernes will be in the fridge next to a carton of milk from cows that eat nothing but grass without any difference in packaging between the products. By the same definition a steer fattened in a feedlot for 60 days on imported GM soy and GM corn could be slaughtered and its meat sold without a word about GM on the pack. Years of drought in Australia have made it more cost-effective for some owners of feed lots to import feeds from foreign nations, with a considerable percentage of the feed being GM. The same economics and labelling situation applies to the chicken, pig and farmed fish industries. There is also a 1 percent tolerance for GM ingredients allowed in foods before they need to be labelled and additives under 1 percent do not need to be declared.

DEAR CONSUMERS ...

With so much uncertainty about foods in the market place big food companies such as Goodman Fielder, bakers of bread and makers of margarine, have very publicly reassured an uneasy public that they do not and will not use GM foods in a letter to all state ministers of agriculture. Supermarket chains, sensing customers' concerns over food provenance, have made very public announcements on GM foods. Woolworths takes one in every three shopping dollars spent on food and groceries nationally through its more than

900 supermarkets operating under Woolworths and Safeway trade names. It has highlighted its concerns over the labelling of GM products, particularly in association with the 'highly refined' loophole and have called for clear 'labelling of all GM ingredients in food products to protect the interests of our customers and to enable informed decision-making'. Its opposition, Coles, has a policy of not using GM ingredients in its house brand but has stated it feels the present labelling is sufficient. Coles was recently taken over by Wesfarmers, a company that also produces agricultural chemicals. Greenpeace's GM campaigner Louise Sales says that, with the moratoria lifted in New South Wales and Victoria, 'There's going to be a large influx of GM canola, which is going to make its way unlabelled and unwanted into the food chain'. As most food manufacturing occurs in these two states, unlabelled GM derived foods will spread nationally even into the states with GM planting bans. The plantings of GM canola were in no way out of the blue. They were the culmination of nearly a decade and a half of lobbying and pressure from GM seed and chemical companies and farming interest groups on government at both the state and federal level.

WHOSE SIDE IS WHO ON?

The culture of Australian government is ostensibly pro-GM. The Commonwealth Scientific and Industrial Research Organisation, a government funded research body that works closely with and accepts funding from industry, has been actively promoting GM foods and stating that, 'Public concern about genetically modified (or transgenic) food is unfounded,' and that, 'Designer produce may be safer than food produced by conventional breeding techniques'. FSANZ, the body responsible for food safety in Australia and New Zealand, refutes statements and research questioning the safety of GM foods.

When the new Labor (centre-left) federal government was elected in November 2007, there was a feeling that perhaps the politics of GM in Australia would move too. A pre-election statement made by the party reads that 'safe and beneficial standards (for GM foods) must be established beyond reasonable doubt...' Months later the new Labor Federal Agriculture Minister was enthusiastically supporting the dropping of the GM crop ban by New South Wales and Victoria, welcoming their decision to allow farmers to grow GM crops. 'I can see some really good opportunities with respect to agriculture for GM food, and the research and development in these areas will have to be part of the changes that need to be driven, if we are going to have people properly prepared for climate change.' With drought gripping the fertile south of Australia, the idea that the GM technology purportedly helping farmers survive climate change is very appealing to many. But Future Farm Industries CRC CEO Kevin Goss has warned that genetically modifying plants for drought tolerance would take more time and money. 'Farmers should look to perennial grasses and strategic mowing to cope with drought conditions,' he said. The way the GM game plays out in Australia is has yet to unfold. The public is caught in an information maelstrom. On one side are the complicit government agencies, well organized farm groups pushing the 'GM is green' mantra and outspoken university academics all advocating an embrace of a GM food future. On the other side are various opposition groups offering a variety of anti-GM messages and suffering a lack of funds. In the middle is a confused population, noted more for its love of sport than of politics, being fed information through a media that prevaricates between hysteria and complacency. The argument at present is over science and economics with the public being asked to take sides. What is missing in the GM debate in Australia is a discussion of what sort of food future the people want.

When Two Elephants Fight

Madieng Seck
Senegal, a journalist of the Journalistes en Afrique
pour le Développement et l'Environnement network
and editor of the *Agri Infos* monthly

The supporters of GMOs forget that the disastrous situation facing West African agriculture is associated with bad agricultural policies. There has been a lack of agrarian reforms in support of female work, inadequate efforts to improve soil fertilization, no credit for thousands of small farmers in family farms, and no promotion of traditional knowledge.

GMO

✕ A lively controversy over the use of genetically modified organisms divides Western Africa. For those in favor, GMOs provide an opportunity to achieve a 'Green Revolution' which can defeat hunger and poverty. For those against, they are a real danger.

'We are in favour of GMOs and new biotechnologies', declared Amadou Moustafa Djigo, President of the Union Nationale Interprofessionnelle des Semences du Sénégal (UNIS) in an interview with *Agri Infos*.

Together with Mr Djigo, there are many Africans who support the use of transgenic plants in agriculture. They state that biotechnologies enable better yields and the prospect of larger stocks of cotton, soy, maize, rice, which can help combat hunger and poverty in areas where agriculture has not yet achieved satisfactory results. Rice cultivation, for example, achieves yields significantly below world averages: less than 1.5 tons per hectare compared to 3.84.

CHRONIC HUNGER

West Africa—which almost completely coincides with the Sahel—is also one of the regions in the world to record a reduction in food output relative to demographic trends. According to a study of the UN World Food Program, one third of the 300 million people living in the area of the Economic Community Of West African States (CEDEAO) are 'chronically threatened by hunger'.

For these reasons, countries such as Burkina Faso, Ivory Coast, Benin, Mali, Niger, Senegal, Togo and Guinea-Bissau have made efforts since 2006 to introduce GM crops, as part of the West Africa Regional Biosafety Program (PRBAO). This initiative, supported by the World Bank and the Global Environment Facility, is implemented by the West African Economic and Monetary Union.

BT COTTON

But while we wait for a common position to be reached, Bt cotton—it owes its name to the mutated gene of *Bacillus thu-*ringiensis, which enables the plant to produce a toxin lethal to parasite larvae—has been tested since 2003 in Burkina Faso, and commercial crops have been grown since last year. It is no secret: Burkina Faso, through its Institut National de Recherche Agronomique (INERA) has entered into a contractual agreement with Monsanto and Sygenta, the two largest agrochemical multinationals, which are vigorously lobbying in this part of Africa. The important point is that cotton accounts for 50 percent of the country's total exports. According to studies carried out by INERA, Bt cotton improves yields by 40 percent, particularly when the transgenic variety Bollgard 2 is used. 'We are sure that biotechnology applied to cultivating cotton can be one of the solutions to the problems of competitiveness,' wrote Professor Alassan Séré, President of the Burkina Biotech Association, in his editorial published in *Biotech Echo* in May 2007. Benin, Ivory Coast, Ghana, Mali and Togo have followed the example of Burkina Faso, deciding in June 2006 to accept cultivation of Bt cotton. According to unconfirmed reports the Senegalese company Sodéfitex, which manages cotton crops in the south of the country, is considering following the example of Burkina Faso.

GM WELL-BEING

Supporters of GMOs think that West African states should quickly adopt these transgenic plants to allow these countries to escape the cycles of poor harvests which cause small farmers lost earnings, hunger and poverty. It is a disastrous situation afflicting both people and animals. This is exactly what is happening this year in Senegal, where low rainfall in 2007, insufficient seed and a lack of fertilizers, water and pesticides have led to a 60 percent collapse in cereal production, particularly affecting millet and corn. The supporters of GMOs claim that transgenic seeds would have withstood these difficulties more successfully. Reinforcing this point of view, Djigo, President of UNIS and West African representative at the African Seed Trade Association (AFSTA), emphasizes that biotechnology brings 'well-being' to Africans. 'But', he continues ' it must be accompanied by a biosafety system which can evaluate the environmental impact of GMOs on humans and animals'.

BAD POLICIES

The supporters of GMOs forget however that the disastrous situation facing West African agriculture is associated with bad agricultural policies. There has been a lack of agrarian reforms in support of female labor, inadequate efforts to improve soil fertilization, no credit for thousands of small farmers in family farms, and no promotion of traditional knowledge.

We should also remember that there are some uncertainties surrounding the consumption of transgenic foods. While cultivation of GM corn in the countries mentioned is still on an experimental basis, this is not the case for the consumption of other transgenic products. In fact, countries such as Brazil or Argentina, well-known for being among the world's largest producers of GM crops, export significant quantities of transgenic wheat, corn, soy and other products to West Africa. Never mind the environmental damage and human and animal health.

PROPERTY TO PROTECT

The opponents of GMOs base their rejection on evidence of disasters caused by these biotechnology products and appeal to precautionary and protection principles. For these opponents—researchers, ecologists and producers belonging to small farmer organizations such as ROPPA in West Africa—transgenic plants constitute a danger to the African continent. The Coalition for the Protection of African Genetic Heritage (COPAGEN) shares this position and is campaigning against the introduction of GMOs to Africa. Through its actions, COPAGEN wants to bring the problem to the attention of African political authorities, and at the same time raise public awareness through widespread information.

Those opposed to GMOs feel laws must be passed to protect The African genetic heritage and to control the risks of environmental pollution. With membership of the World Trade Organisation, it is possible to envisage a risk that African countries could become dependent on GM seeds. Then there are some plant varieties which specifically belong to particular African rural communities and should be protected. One representative example is fonio (Digitaria exilis), a cereal with a minute grain, which is gluten-free and well tolerated by diabetics. If we do not protect ourselves against the problems that can arise from the use of GMOs or intellectual property issues connected with seeds, we risk exposing Africa to many dangers and its small farmers to the possibility of losing some of their rights.

GIANTS

We should at this point mention the World Trade Organisation's Agreement on Trade Related Aspects of Intellectual Property Rights (TRIPS). Following this agreement, since 2002 the countries of the West African Economic and Monetary Union (UEMOA) and Economic Community of West African States (CEDEAO) have tried to harmonize their laws covering the use or non-use of GMOs in their countries.

The former Senegalese Minister for Scientific Research, Yaye Kéne Gassama, while chairing a meeting of his CEDEAO colleagues in January 2007, stated: 'Most countries have followed the Cartagena Protocol on Biosafety in their legislation, but they must each be fully aware of the issues and express their own opinion. Technology transfer must not conceal and override ethical issues'.

It must now be recognized however that some West African countries have difficulty in harmonizing their intended actions in the context of globalization. At present, we are not witnessing a simple debate on the issue of GMOs, but a real battle between the United States and the European Union. Africa should keep its distance from this battle of giants, looking for its own alternative way. As Julius Nyerere, former president of Tanzania said: 'When two elephants fight, it is the grass that suffers'.

The Battle in Catalonia

Francesc Balañá
Spain, journalist with the daily newspaper *La Mañana*

The food and pharmaceutical use of stevia is not permitted in Europe except for a few countries. The only reason for this is because it offers real prospects for improving the quality of life for ill people and is not covered by patents, thereby constituting a risk to the interests of pharmaceutical companies.

GMO

In three years the Terres de Lleida Convivium has become one of the main opponents of transgenic products in its efforts to defend a range of local quality products. The convivium, comprising people with a variety of backgrounds, has managed to persuade the public authorities to promote alternative forms of agriculture. Nonetheless, Catalonia continues to be the second most important region in Europe for the cultivation of transgenic products, with the nearby autonomous region of Aragon coming first. In little more than five years, the coverage of GM corn grown in Catalonia has increased from 6,000 to 20,000 hectares, making organic agriculture ever more difficult.

This situation has prompted Slow Food, together with other agricultural associations and consortia, to organize a petition to force the Catalan government to debate this controversial question in regional parliament. The 50,000 signatures needed to present a bill for a GM-free Catalonia have almost been collected (www.somloquesembrem.org).

MY PRECIOUS SEEDS

The end objective is to transform Catalonia into a region without any transgenic crops. Farmer Josep Pàmies, leader of the Balaguer convivium and activist in the local anti-GM campaign, knows that this will be difficult to achieve: multinationals will defend their position with every economic means at their disposal, forgetting, as they always do, aspects connected to health. As Pàmies tells us, multinationals are keen for farmers to be forced to buy transgenic seeds from them each year, subject to their conditions. We should remember that in the past farmers gathered seeds from their own crops, avoiding extra costs and remaining free from dependence on large-scale agribusiness.

When it comes to effects on human health, Pàmies adds that the use of transgenic products can cause pathologies which may not be life-threatening, but can become chronic. In other words, they can generate dependence on medication for a person's whole life. These diseases are a goldmine for pharmaceutical companies, also large multinationals, for whom money is obviously more important than protecting health.

STEVIA

We can see another example in the ban on the use of stevia (*Stevia rebaudiana Bertoni*). This is a plant originally from Paraguay, which because of its sweetening power 200 times greater than sugar—but without providing calories or altering blood glucose levels—can be used by diabetics with obvious benefit. The food and pharmaceutical use of stevia is not permitted in Europe except for a few countries. The only reason for this is because it offers real prospects for improving the quality of life for ill people and is not covered by patents, thereby constituting a risk to the interests of pharmaceutical companies. Through the efforts of Slow Food, information about the plant's properties is being disseminated and prompting growing public interest.

Stevia can be sold as an ornamental plant: this is the legal loophole identified by Slow Food, which allows anyone to have it at home. It is not an ideal solution but this is how things stand, and the plant's reputation is spreading across the country. The objective is to obtain authorization so it can be used for culinary and pharmaceutical use, as is the case in three quarters of the world. Members of the Terres de Lleida Convivium do not think this is enough however: they are sure stevia has additional unknown uses and want further research to be carried out. This is why stevia has become the Slow Food organization's emblem in the Lleida region: the snail and the plant share and symbolize the association's basic principles. Such ideas are becoming more common in Catalonia and Spain. Josep Pàmies welcomes to his farm anyone wanting to find out more about the properties of stevia or who is aware of the importance of reviving local food products—which focus on flavor rather than appearance—and in the past ensured autonomy and identity for farmers.

VARIETIES PROTECTED

Ever increasing numbers of people are becoming aware of these issues and sharing Slow Food's position. The association's message is welcomed and promoted through the media. However Josep Pàmies reports that some large TV broadcasters have come to his farm and recorded programs, but they have never been broadcast. When Josep asked why, the answer was: 'We didn't get permission'. Pàmies feels that this is due to the dependence of mass media on the advertising system. Positive news about the effects of stevia would adversely affect the interests of major advertisers, who pay significant sums of money to TV stations.

Slow Food Terres de Lleida not only organizes meetings for members, but also puts on frequent public events. Its ongoing constructive efforts mean that the public is properly informed of the association's message. Only three years ago the Terres de Lleida Convivium began to spread the word about its activities; it is now well-known and everyone knows what it is fighting for. The ideals it expresses are gaining greater acceptance than expected, because people want to return to a different style of eating and a different way of defining health. GMOs and laboratory products are provoking growing suspicion and this is sure to highlight the slow philosophy. Local authorities are also showing their interest, particularly La Noguera District Council, which together with Slow Food has begun to recover endangered native plant varieties. In addition to propagating and providing farmers with recovered plants, this initiative will also revive and collect the knowledge which has allowed these plants to be cultivated for so many years. The Catalonian Regional Government's Department of Agriculture, Food and Rural Action has realized the importance of promoting research to help improve the public's quality of life and as part of this, Slow Food has been given space at the Vallfogona de Balaguer Agricultural College. The aim is to collect native varieties, particularly fruit and vegetables but also trees, which are at risk of extinction. This is highly significant since public authorities have never before shown interest in issues of this kind. It is a first step which may indicate a change of course for current policies.

For both the general public and government organizations, Slow Food is seen as an organization that can effect the changes needed so people can live better lives, from economic, ethical and health perspectives.

UK Doubts

Joanna Blythman
UK, Edinburgh-based journalist and food writer

The retailer Marks & Spencer even guarantees that none of its meat, dairy or eggs come from livestock fed on genetically-modified cereals. However, the biotech lobby now senses a new opportunity to represent GM food to an unwilling public by exploiting fears about rising food prices and global food shortages.

GMO

For over a decade now, GM food has met with intense opposition in the UK from both consumers and environmentalists. At a landmark event in the Savoy in London in 1999, 150 of Britain's top food writers and chefs, in partnership with Greenpeace, launched 'Food Writers Against GM Food'. The anti-GM message was taken up by the influential newspaper *The Daily Mail*, which ran lists of GM foods that could be on sale, unlabelled, on supermarket shelves. Public concern became acute and, almost overnight, the supermarkets took fright and started delisting products with GM ingredients and those made using GM processes. Since then, public opposition has hardened. A recent government consultation found that 95 percent of Britons don't want to eat GM food. Dino Adriano, a former chief executive for a supermarket chain, has recently gone on record as saying that 'GM is invasive, and if allowed to develop freely, will deny alternative choices for ever to those who wish to avoid it .... I remain doubtful that such a fundamental step should ever be taken'. Even with steeply rising prices, any UK chain embracing GM food would be committing commercial folly.

PROFIT AND PREOCCUPATION

The food industry and retailers are doing rather nicely out of the growth in organic and ethical foods and are not at all keen to get involved with a campaign that giant pharmaceutical companies have fought and lost. Any company that embraces this controversial technology would send out all the wrong messages in the UK and put red hazard warning lights around its brand. The status quo is that food retailers are keen to disassociate themselves from GM food. The retailer Marks & Spencer even guarantees that none of its meat, dairy or eggs come from livestock fed on genetically-modified cereals. However, the biotech lobby now senses a new opportunity to represent GM food to an unwilling public by exploiting fears about rising food prices and global food shortages. As his parting shot before retiring from his post, the government's Chief Scientist, Sir David King, went on the high-profile Radio 4 *Today* programme to argue that GM food would feed the world and save the planet. In the habitual manner, he dismissed opponents of GM as irrational hysterics stumbling around in a sea of superstition, and also had a go at the media for listening to them. Then he went on to give listeners a patronising pep talk about how GM food could feed the world and save the planet, offering up the supposed example of crop trials around Lake Victoria in Kenya. One week on, Sir David had egg on his face when his office had to admit that these trials did not involve the use of GM technology at all. Quite the opposite, in fact. This successful project actually uses green farming methods—a sort of companion planting approach—using plants that can be cultivated alongside food crops to naturally boost yields. Researchers identified one set of plants that naturally deters parasitic weeds, while another, a species of grass, attracts the pests. Known as a the 'Push-pull Project', this is in fact a glowing example of how simple, cheap crop management can achieve results, without any of the potential health and environmental impacts of genetic modification or pesticides.

SAFE GOVERNMENTS

Environmentalists continue to put pressure on government over GM. The Food Standards Agency has been forced to declare that illegal GM rice from China found in the UK food chain is 'unsafe' and belatedly told food companies to recall any affected products, following a court case brought against it by Friends of the Earth. First the Blair and now the Brown (Labour) governments, however, have sought to encourage GM and develop the UK biotech sector. Proposals for Britain set no separation time between growing a GM and non-GM crop, although 95 percent of public respondents to DEFRA's consultation opposed that, saying that this would lead to unavoidable contamination of the food chain. Further evidence of this risk emerged recently with the news that Swedish researchers have found that GM crops can persist in the soil for at least ten years. So environmentalists are demanding that the government implement tough rules to protect GM-free food and farming from contamination, along with a strengthening of environmental liability laws to force biotech companies to stump up for any damage they cause to the environment or farmers'

livelihoods. GM companies steadfastly resist all measures to make them financially responsible for any contamination to conventional or organic crops by GM escapees. Nevertheless, environment minister Phil Woolas has it that 'GM crops may be approved for cultivation here in the future, if they pass the rigorous [sic!] safety assessment procedure that is in place'.

AUTONOMOUS TRASH

This puts him on a collision course with the devolved governments of Wales and Scotland. Wales currently has GM-free status and new proposals by the Welsh Assembly Government will protect this by effectively banning genetically modified crops from the region by applying a strict 'polluter pays' principle that will put an end even to trial plantings. The proposals, which are supported by the Farmers' Union of Wales, make GM companies and the farmers who plant GM crops legally liable for contamination or 'genetic trespass' – even if they have a licence and even if scientific knowledge at the time leads them to believe the material was harmless. In Scotland, the SNP government's clear position is that it intends to resolutely maintain the current moratorium on planting GM crops in Scotland. 'GM crops are not grown in Scotland and we believe this respects the wishes of Scottish consumers who want local, high quality produce. Scotland has a wonderful and varied environment, rich in biodiversity and we do not wish to jeopardise this,' says Environment Minister, Mike Russell.

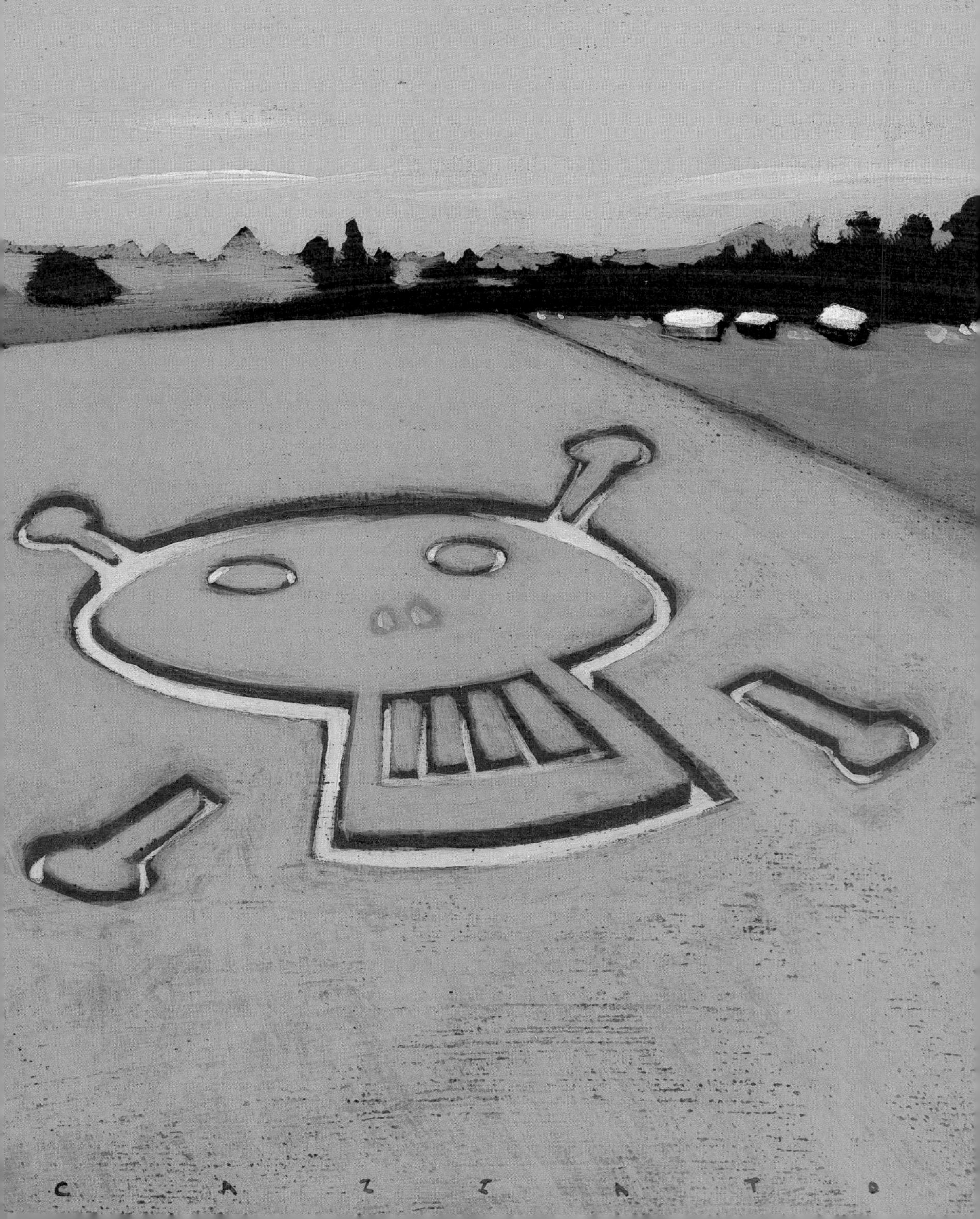
C A Z Z A T O

Insecurity and Death

Alexander Baranov
Russia, geneticist and president of the National
Asociation for Genetic Safety in Moscow

On April 15 2008, for the first time in its history, the UNO actually condemned the use of the genetically modified technologies in agriculture because, as it stated in its report, they do not solve the problem of hunger for millions of people, but at once pose a threat to human health and the future of the whole planet.

GMO

The problem of the biological safety of the food market and the creation of a system capable of ensuring this safety has become a major issue not only in Russia, but also in other countries of the world. It is connected with the global character of the active physical, chemical, and now also genetic pollution of Mother Earth that results in an intensive accumulation of harmful substances in agricultural products at all stages of their production, and that later appears in the products we eat.

The contamination of the environment is not the only reason for the increase in the content of dangerous substances in food products. A lot of growth hormone stimulants, antibiotics and other agents are given to animals, birds and fish, and as organisms adapt to them, so the dose is increased. All these agents might appear on our plates. Nowadays there are many special technologies that help to prolong the life of a product and make it more attractive to the customer, and producers do not care much about the possible negative influence of these 'convenient' agents on people's health. Meanwhile, the number of artificial chemically-synthesized coloring agents, preservatives, emulsifiers, flavorings, sweeteners and other additives is constantly growing.

UNO CONDEMNATION

The creation and the usage of GMOs have proved to be another problem that has already exerted a strong influence on the political, economic and social processes of society, the food safety of many countries, the environment and biodiversity. Unfortunately, mankind is witnessing the hasty application of scientific achievements for commercial purposes: without necessary, thorough biological safety control they have been used in agriculture and in food production. We might say that nowadays transnational biotech and agri-food companies are carrying out a secret experiment on mankind.

International organizations such as the UNO, FAO, WHO, UNESCO, NATO, INTERPOL, the World Bank and others have realized the scale of the oncoming catastrophe. On April 15 2008, for the first time in its history, the UNO actually condemned the use of the genetically modified technologies in agriculture because, as it stated in its report, they do not solve the problem of hunger for millions of people, but at once pose a threat to human health and the future of the whole planet. There is growing concern, moreover, that the development of GMOs will lead to a monopolization of agricultural resources, while, at the same time, it is necessary to make such resources available to various strata of the population to overcome famine. UNO representatives suggest development in other directions in so far as the world should not concentrate only on biotechnology and on GMOs. Experts are encouraging the world community to pay more attention to selection experiments and to ecological agriculture.

CULTIVATION BANNED

So what is the situation in Russia? As far as its attitude towards GMOs is concerned, Russia is no exception to common international processes and is currently witnessing a struggle between supporters and opponents of GMOs. Supporters of GMOs are involved in different lobby activities, seeking to ease and to 'blur' the confines of the Russian bio-safety laws. Their actions aim to facilitate the promotion of the interests of transnational biotech, pharmaceutical and food companies at all levels of agricultural production and in adjacent sectors, including pharmaceutical production.

The other party is not against biotechnology if it is carried out at scientific level. The impossibility of cultivating or using GM-cultures in Russia is evident due to many factors, among which the present level of scientific development in general and genetic engineering in particular, the imperfection of GMOs themselves, the weak scientific and technological base of bio-safety control, the ambiguity of all potential and remote risks connected with the use of GMOs.

In Russian fields there are no GMOs although their cultivation is not prohibited by law. Not a single modified plant has passed the specific legal procedure for registration and permission to grow GM crops. But the use of GMOs is authorized, and there are 16 officially accepted plants and 5 microorganisms: transgenic soya, corn, sugar beet, potato and rice.

0.9 PERCENT LIMIT

The legislative base for biological safety is developing fast. Non-governmental organizations participated in the formulation of the Biosafety Federal Law. In order to regulate the turnover, usage and control of transgenic raw material, GM food and forage on Russian territory, a number of technical protocols, national standards, specifications and rules have been created and, in some cases, already function.

The Russian Federation consumer protection law requires compulsory labeling of all products containing more than 0.9 percent of transgenic elements. The limit was introduced last November, while prior to that the same article envisaged compulsory labeling of all goods containing any measurable quantity of GM ingredients. The first version of the law was supported by practically all ecological and consumer non-governmental organizations. They now think that the introduction of the limit on quantity confuses the consumer and de facto has nothing to do with people's health. As long as the question of the safety of GM products for people's health remains open on a world scale and the GM ingredients in products are not subject to high-level research, non-governmental organizations and a group of scientists propose to undertake the following actions: to temporarily suspend the use of all permitted GMOs in Russia until the results of new state-managed and independent researches are received, and to invoke a temporary moratorium on the registration of new GMOs; to initiate a recheck of the biological safety of the 16 GM-cultures that have been already registered and permitted on the territory of the Russian Federation; to carry out a compulsory biosafety control on each GM-culture, testing it on five generations of mammals to establish the remote consequences of its influence.

The above-mentioned points were reflected in the joint motion of the non-governmental organizations and the scientists addressed to the chairman of the Russian Federation Government Office and the Chief Medical Sanitation Officer of Russia last November.

FREE FROM ...

Worldwide discussion of the problem and the absence of a single government opinion about the problem of GMOs has caused public opinion and in some cases local authorities to have regional legislative acts and norms passed regulating the turnover and use of GMOs. The Moscow, Belgorod, Kurgan, Kostroma, Sverdlovsk and Murmansk regions, the Krasnoyarsk and Krasnodar territories and some others are now called GMO-free, with some of the regional legislative acts forbidding the use of state subsidies to purchase the GM raw materials and products for social needs (for children and school canteens, for hospitals and preventive treatment centers).

As a whole, Russia has not yet defined its attitude towards GMOs. According to the results of a survey, 86 percent of the population is against the cultivation of transgenic cultures, 73 percent against the use of GMOs in products and 98 percent against their use in baby food.

ECOLOGICAL FUTURE

As a party to the Convention on Biological Diversity, Russia has not ratified the Cartagena Protocol on Biosafety, though it has actively participated in its discussion. In the meantime, the lengthy talks and the government's unclear position on the question, the imperfection of Russian biosafety legislation, the official disunity of the supervising bodies and their technical incompetence and the absence of customs barriers for GMOs are contributing to allow transgenic products easy access to the territory of the Russian Federation. All these factors and others besides are adding to the confusion reigning on the Russian food market, increasing the vulnerability of citizens and raising tension in society.

Recent research by domestic and foreign experts in the field of agricultural economics has proved that for the next 60 years Russia could become a potential leader and supplier of ecological products to the world food market. The positioning of Russia as a GMO-free country on the international agricultural market, combined with the development of ecological agriculture, might prove to be a strategically important step in securing Russian leadership of the international movement for the 'ecologization' of food production. Such a role would certainly be widely supported by European countries and by the developing nations of Southeast Asia, Africa and South America.

NEW CREATIVE SPACES

George Ritzer
USA, Professor of Sociology at the University of Maryland and author
of numerous books and essays

GLOBAL/LOCAL

The idea of creative destruction has received a great deal of attention since it was first created in 1942 by the economist Joseph Schumpeter (1883-1950). In fact, it is probably the most famous metaphor employed in work on economic phenomena. What is interesting about all the attention to creative destruction is that Schumpeter actually said very little about that idea. His most famous and useful statement on it is the following in which he argues that it is the process 'that incessantly revolutionizes the economic structure *from within*, incessantly destroying the old one, incessantly creating a new one. This process of Creative Destruction is the essential fact of about capitalism. It is what capitalism consists in and what every capitalist concern has got to live in'.

OUT WITH THE OLD

It seems clear that one of the things Slow Food and other 'alter-globalization' international Non-Governmental Organizations are seeking to do is to combat this kind of blind faith in creative destruction and to find a viable alternative to it that deals with its worst excesses. The blind faith associated with the idea of creative destruction is that destruction will inevitably lead to creation of the new. That is, the old must be cleared away to make room for the new and that once that space has been made available, the new will necessarily follow. There are various problems associated with this view with the result that it might be better to think in terms of 'destructive creativity', or even plain 'destruction'. Schumpeter was writing in an era before modern globalization. Thus, his focus was within a given nation-state and the idea that, within that geographic space, what one area might lose (at least in the short-run) through destruction, would either be regained in that space at some later date or gained in some other part of the nation more-or-less simultaneous with the loss. If true (and it certainly was not always, or perhaps even usually, true), it was a comforting scenario within each nation-state since loss led sooner or later, or perhaps even both, to gains, perhaps even gains of a greater magnitude than the losses due to destruction.

MODERN DISTANCES

As problematic as this scenario was in the pre-globalization era, it is even more problematic today in the 'global age'. The reason is that even if we accept the most basic premise of the theory of creative destruction, that which is destroyed may well occur in one part of the world while that which is created, assuming it occurs, may be found half way around the world. This balance might be of some consolation from the point of the globe as a whole, but it is of little solace to those who live in areas that have encountered destruction and may well never experience any creativity; they may experience permanent destruction.

Operating in the global age, and perhaps even given impetus by globalization, it seems to me that what Slow Food seeks to do is, at least in part, to protect the 'local' from de-

struction in the face of new 'creations', likely elsewhere in the world. Thus, it seeks to protect local ways of growing and raising food in the face of the destruction threatened by industrial farms that may be thousands of miles away; local ways of eating and local restaurants in the face of threats posed by global chains headquartered in other parts of the globe; local, handmade ways of preparing foods endangered by globally uniform and industrialized methods; and locally grown ingredients as opposed to those that are mass manufactured at central locations and distributed globally.

LOCAL FORMS

However, Slow Food is not just about protecting the local from destruction, but also about creation at the local as well as at the global levels. At the local level it is about the creation of new types of crops, new ways of preparing food (as long as it is handmade), the use of new types of ingredients and new ways of combining them, new local shops and restaurants, and so on. At the global level, its focus is on creating a new global type of organization based on local convivia. Certainly, the Ark of Taste, the annual Slow Food awards, and Terra Madre are global derivatives of Slow Food that are creative in themselves and that seek to not only protect the local but create new local forms.

Slow Food may not have had the idea of creative destruction in mind when it was created, or as it has evolved. It has clearly been shaped, if unknowingly, in opposition to some of the basic principles, and worst abuses, of creative destruction. Furthermore, formed during the early years of the 'global age', it has been, again implicitly, aware of the additional dangers posed by creative destruction in a global context, as well as the related, but more general dangers, posed by neo-liberal economic globalization which is very cognizant and supportive of creative destruction as an important, if not absolutely central, underlying principle.

FOTO N. RAPETTI

SLOW FOOD AT THE LOCAL LEVEL IS ABOUT THE CREATION OF NEW TYPES OF CROPS, NEW WAYS OF PREPARING FOOD, THE USE OF NEW TYPES OF INGREDIENTS, NEW LOCAL SHOPS AND RESTAURANTS.

FOTO N. RAPETTI

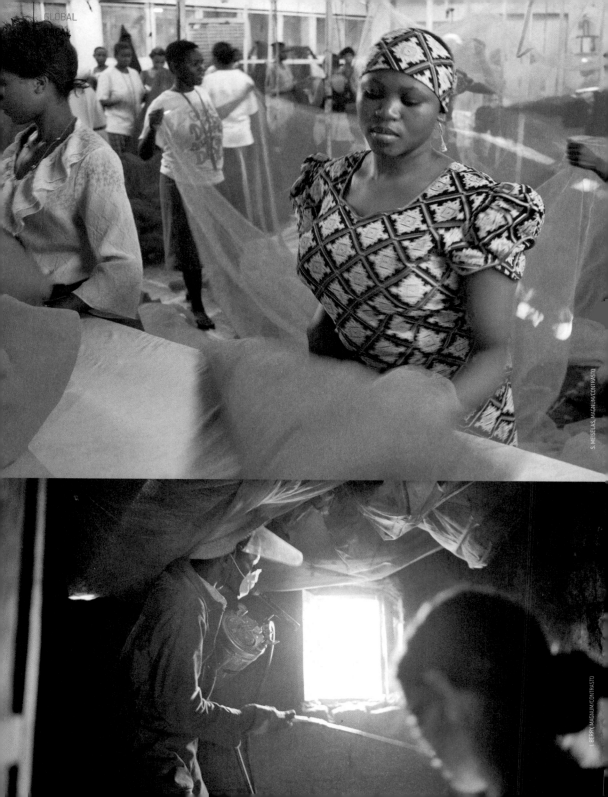

THE DREAM WE NEED

Serge Latouche
France, Emeritus Professor
of Economic Sciences at the University of Paris

GLOBAL/LOCAL

In the small Pyrenean village where I have spent part of every year for the last 40, I surprised a neighbor spraying the land in front of his house. 'What are you spraying?' I asked, fearing the worst—maybe he was using Monsanto's Roundup, the herbicide favored by amateur gardeners. 'It's a weedkiller,' he answered. 'I 've no idea which. It's one they sell in Prades.'[1] It would be interesting of course to investigate the concept of 'weeds', the result of a vision of a somewhat special and typically western vision of the mastery of Nature, but for the moment I limited myself to the problem at hand. 'Do you realize,' I asked him, 'that that stuff contains all sorts of crap that's dangerous for you and for the environment?' 'Oh!' he replied. 'With all the toxic products around these days, we're fucked up anyway. So this stuff isn't going to make any difference. Why make such a fuss?' It's pointless explaining to a passive consumer that, if you want to kill weeds at all costs, there are mechanical or thermal systems, all perfectly effective, that, unlike your Gaucho[2] or your Paraquat[3] or other persistent, carcinogenic and reprotoxic organic pollutants produced and nonchalantly distributed by Bayer, Novartis, Syngenta, Aventis, and Basf, are either totally harmless or harmful to an infinitely less extent.

RESIGNATION

It is surely considering this refusal to resist, this slipshod way of doing things at all levels of society—from the 'decent guy' I described above to the Prince's technocratic advisor (be he right-wing or left)—that the writer Georges Bernanos declared that 'Realism is the clear conscience of scoundrels'. It's true, realism is to accept the world for what it is, to live with disaster and resign yourself to it, with the excuse that the only future that the dominant lines of force draw is the protraction of current trends. As Michel Dias said so effectively, these realists prefer 'a fatal outcome but a certain one, rather than the uncertainty of a future entrusted to human initiative'.

When conscientious objectors are accused of utopianism, it is precisely on account of their opposition to this kind of realism. We effectively swim against the tide. We refuse to succumb to the diktats of the present situation, to the tyranny of TINA,[4] which limits being to the actual. The positive utopia we claim for ourselves excludes the refusal of other possible worlds. When we say that there is another world and that, according to the formulation of Paul Eluard, it is to be found precisely in what we know, we accept the possible of being. This being is not confined to the lethal developments of market economy logics, but also contemplates a way out of the economy, an escape route towards a society and a civilization that are emancipated and autonomous. Accusing us of chasing chimeras is totally unfair. Now we know that the generalization of development is impossible. Hence it is letting oneself go to the suicidal logic of the society of growth and westernization that represents a utopia in the negative sense of the term. This realist aptitude of 'scoundrels' makes manifest the odd yearning for catastrophes that unconsciously assails the West and of which, in France, Jacques Attali—at once author of *Une brève histoire de l'avenir*,[5] a gloomy diagnosis of the future of humanity, and of a report on proposals to 'free growth'—is a caricature.

HOPE

The desire for catastrophe that the Prince's advisor and my neighbor testify to so well is entirely different from what I have defined the 'pedagogy of catastrophes'. In the first case, catastrophe is as denied as it is assumed as an ineluctable justification for doing nothing;

in the second, it is taken seriously to learn from accidents that could not be avoided and evade the threat of the apocalypse that 'realists' are preparing for us.

A realism of this kind is thus the exact opposite of utopia as we understand it. The degrowth project is precisely the source of hope, of the dream we need to evade the misery of the present. It is possible to repeat, word by word, what the economist Gustave Massiah, one of the founders of Attac Francia, says about the 'other world' project: 'It may be regarded as utopian, but a utopia may be the reality of tomorrow. It is built as a concrete utopia and serves as a reference for new ideals and a new possible. And it already influences the reality of today thanks to the action of the movements that refer to it'. Thus, far from finding refuge in the unreal, the degrowth project seeks to explore the objective possibilities of the given situation and to fight to make them become reality.

Article taken from the French weekly *Politis*, close to movements and campaigns for a fair economy. Bernard Langlois, the magazine's founder, is a member of the anti-globalization association ATTAC.

Note

1. Town in the western Pyrenees, in the Languedoc-Roussillon region.
2. Range of herbicides and insecticides produced by Bayer.
3. Non-selective herbicide.
4. The acronym TINA (*There Is No Alternative*) refers to a slogan attributed to the former British premier Margaret Thatcher, who argued that there was no alternative to capitalism.
5. *A Brief History of the Future*, Fayard, 2006.

THE DEGROWTH PROJECT IS A SOURCE OF HOPE, THE DREAM WE NEED TO ESCAPE THE MISERY OF THE PRESENT.

LEICHT-
VERPACKUNGEN
ALBA
SERVICE | MIT SYSTEM
0180 - 351 82 351*
www.alba.info
LEICHT-
VERPACKUNGEN
ALBA

©ALBA AG

ALBA
SERVICE | MIT SYSTEM
www.alba.info
ALBA
Actros

ZERO WASTE

Robin Murray
UK, industrial economist at the London School of Economics

GLOBAL/LOCAL

Waste is the shadow side of the economy, the untouchable in the caste system of commodities. Stripped of desire, it weighs like a corpse around the necks of the living. It is placed in black bags or bins, and transported, like the dead, to sites of exclusion—to landfills and incinerators that are the graveyards and crematoria in the kingdom of objects.

From the perspective of policy, waste has first and foremost been seen as an issue of public health, something that needs to be removed from society as quickly and cheaply as possible. What developed in response has been a system of mass disposal, where household waste is set out, collected and disposed of as a single stream of mixed waste. Scale and speed have been everything. Collection lorries have got bigger, compactors more powerful, incinerators and landfills larger and larger. Mass production generated as its counterpart mass waste and a Fordist waste industry.

MODERN LEVIATHAN

Mass waste was not simply the discards of mass consumption. It also comprised the waste generated at each phase of production, in mines or fields, in factories and shops, all of which far exceeded consumer waste. In England producers accounted for 91 percent of national waste. With food, for every kilogram we eat, 10 kg of waste are generated along the food chain. For consumer goods the trail of waste can be much greater. A car that weighs a ton takes 70 tonnes of material to produce it. Waste is the leviathan of the modern industrial system.

Over the past 30 years there has been a growing recognition that this system of extensive exploitation of the material world cannot be sustained. It is not just a question of the profligate use of materials.[1] It is also the energy it takes to process the materials and the ever mounting problem of disposal.

In many countries the trigger for change has been political—the opposition by local communities to extraction and logging at one end of the chain and to new landfills and incinerators at the other. But what started as primarily a movement of resistance—sparked in the case of waste by the evidence of the hazardous emissions from waste sites—

time and again has turned into a movement of alternatives.

The case is highlighted by organic waste. In England, of every kilogram of food we buy, we throw one third away. In the pre-modern period much of this would have been composted or given to pigs and chickens—as late as the 1970s some of London's food waste was transported to pig farms in East Anglia and came back to Londoners in the form of the 'Tottenham sausage'. But urbanism and food regulation broke this cycle, and resulted in a double loss. On the one hand the land lost a major source of nutrients, on the other food waste was concentrated in landfills where, coupled with garden and other organic waste, it became a significant contributor to global warming.

COMPOST MADE IN ITALY

As evidence grew about soil degradation and erosion, on the environmental impact of artificial fertilisers and the potential role of compost-improved soils for the prevention of flooding and for the sequestration of carbon, so the pressure rose to restore the biological cycle.[2] In the UK a community composting movement grew up. Municipalities encouraged home composting and introduced green collections. By 200, 3 2 million tonnes of organic waste were being composted at 325 facilities.

Industrial composting systems are now well established in The Netherlands and Germany. But the most striking model—with the highest rates of capture—has been developed in Italy. Municipalities—supported by the innovative agrarian institute in Monza—found that making a separate collection of food waste from households and restaurants, and encouraging home composting, meant that they could both create marketable compost and keep the harmful organic waste away from disposal. Instead of the big black plastic bag, many of the municipalities introduced a small, transparent bio-degradable plastic bag, which could be collected by small (even electric) vehicles and composted close-by. A local biological cycle has been restored. It is a more complex process. Householders have to separate their food waste at the sink. Extra collections and processing are needed. The fact that compost is now a commodity and no longer a waste, means that there has to be scientific testing and quality control, advanced water treatment systems, and marketing specialists, all the things needed by an industry oriented to production rather than destruction. It is also a slower process. It can take 60 days or more to manage food waste in this way, instead of the half-day journey to landfill or incinerator. But it is a journey that creates value out of what would otherwise cause environmental damage and, remarkably, has often done so at lower financial cost to the municipalities. It is the slow waste tortoise that has gained the prize.

GREY ENERGY

In the Italian model, food waste has been made separate and visible. One council was even taken to court by a resident objecting to using transparent plastic bags. But visibility is everything if food waste is to be transformed into a useful material. The same holds true for other waste. The moment waste is removed from the dustbin into the light—and many community groups started by collectively sorting the waste into its many components—it becomes clear that, like food, much of what had been discarded as waste is potentially a source of value. Recyclers in cities now refer to waste as urban mines and urban forests.

More than that, much so-called waste embodied what is called 'grey energy'—the energy used in every stage of production. By the early 1990s, the five leading non food materials in the Western domestic waste stream—paper, cardboard, steel, aluminium, and glass—were found to account for two thirds of industrial electricity use in the US. Rescuing these materials from disposal has meant that the energy needed for virgin materials is no longer needed. An assessment of the ambitious Dutch climate change programme in the 1990s found that half the CO_2 savings came from recycling.

So alongside the restoration of biological cycles, there has been a parallel move to restore material cycles, thereby preserving the value of the materials, the energy, and the work embodied in the discarded commodities. It is a question not just of recycling, but upcycling, of finding ways in which the qualities of the discards can provide more valuable inputs in their next life (crushed bottles as water filters for example, or old tyres into basketball court surfaces). As with food, the perspective involves a shift from the linear model of mass waste to a circular model that conserves value and resources.

The critique of traditional waste systems and the development of alternatives has been led by community and environmental movements. Community recyclers and composters pioneered new systems of collection and processing in Australasia, in Germany, the UK, and in much of North America. In response to their work, local and regional governments started promoting the new policy. They found that quite quickly they were diverting 50 percent or more of household waste from disposal, with some municipalities up to 70 percent and even 80 percent among the pioneers.

TOYOTA METHOD

What was then stopping progress to 100%? The manual sorting of dustbin waste found some items that were technically difficult or very expensive to recycle—like Tetrapaks, and plastic bags. Some are made of unrecyclable compounds, or are hazardous to recycle or re-use. But those are in principle resolvable. So, having progressed that far up the mountain, why not aim for the top? This is the background to the idea of Zero Wa-

ste. It was pioneered by community groups in Australasia in the second half of the 1990s and has spread remarkably in a decade. Not only have many municipalities signed up to Zero Waste, so have regional and state governments, particularly in Federal states—California, Nova Scotia, Victoria, South Australia, and Western Australia. The first country to adopt it is New Zealand. Lebanon and Taiwan have followed and even the Chinese (who now account for one third of the world's garbage) have adopted the principle of the circular economy in their latest Plan. In England there is a Zero Waste Charter, and in 2001 a Zero Waste International was formed as a network of community groups. It is an idea that has caught fire.

Zero Waste was initially both an aspiration and a methodology. As an aspiration it sought to eliminate all waste by restoring the material and biological cycles. In the phrase of the German biochemist Michael Braungart the move is from 'cradle to grave' to 'cradle to cradle'.

As a methodology, it borrowed from many modern industries, including those that were themselves adopting Zero Waste policies, notably the auto sector, electronics, office machinery and chemicals. Toyota which had developed the concept of continuous improvement and zero defects, adopted the principle of zero waste, and cut waste in its assembly operations by 98 percent. Honda, Hewlett Packard, Du Pont, Fuji Xerox, Minolta, NEC, Epson and Interface are others who are committed to Zero Waste.

UNSUSTAINABLE WASTE

In terms of methods it requires all involved in production to identify the origins of waste, to find innovative ways to reduce it and to re-use or recycle that which cannot be prevented.

For household waste this has involved developing very different systems of storage, collection, and sorting. It has meant designing new types of home container, new vehicles, new more complex logistics, and new time patterns of collection—by week, month, and season. To restore the pre-modern biological and material cycles, zero waste has had to adopt postmodern tools. It needs the most advanced methods for handling complexity. The best modern recycling systems use bar codes, on-board weighing, data-based feedback systems and sophisticated incentives. Post-modern recycling is a form of reverse retailing.

But because of its aspirations Zero Waste is also a critique and a programme of economic alternatives. What began as a movement to reclaim recyclable materials led to the questioning of many features of production itself—not just the trail of waste it produced, but its hazards, and its blindness to the need to recycle and re-use. Waste came to be seen as a symptom of an unsustainable system of production and consumption.

And out of the critique has emerged the agenda to redesign current systems of production, distribution and consumption.[3] To reduce waste design has to move to the centre of the stage, and it needs the design industry to move with it. The industry needs to shift its focus from the innovation of surfaces, to a new form of transformation design, the redesign of productive systems and each of the elements within them in line with contemporary environmental imperatives.

How can products and processes be designed that will enable all the 're-s', re-use, reduction, repair, reverse manufacturing, re-skinning, re-refining and reverse engi-neering? How can products be modularised, and commodities leased as part of a service? How can product lives be extended, and be more intensively used? Alongside assembly lines there are now disassembly lines. In local garages there are car share pools. Are these the emerging patterns of a new economy?

Zero Waste has come to these questions from the vantage point of reducing waste. On the way it has met with many others—coming from different places but on a similar track. As with tributaries flowing into the same river, these are currents that are already creating in practice the outlines of different kind of economy, one with greater lightness and fewer shadows.

Notes

1 US material use rose from 200 million tonnes in 1900 to 2.8 billion tonnes by 1990, by which time the world figure had risen to 16 billion tonnes. Asian industrialisation further intensifies the pressure on resources – and on waste generation, with China already accounting for a third of the world's garbage.

2 One of the best recent summaries of the value of compost for improving soil structures and countering environmental degradation is in Appendix 6 of the report by Dominic Hogg, Adrian Gibbs, Enzo Favoino, and Marco Ricci, Managing Biowastes from Households in the UK: Applying Life-cycle Thinking in the Framework of Cost-benefit Analysis, Appendix 6, WRAP, May 2007. Australian evidence suggests that the great value in that climate was in improved water retention in the soil and avoided phosphate depletion.

3 Life cycle analysis and the complex economic and environmental models that build on it, detail each stage and each process that a product passes through, and in doing so issue an invitation to innovate.

Robin Murray, *Zero Waste*, Greenpeace Environmental Trust, London 2002. The book can be downloaded in pdf format from the Greenpeace Australia Pacific and Great Britain websites.
http://www.greenpeace.org/raw/content/australia/resources/reports/toxics/zero-waste-book-by-robin-murra.pdf
http://www.greenpeace.org.uk/media/reports/the-environmental-trust-zero-waste

FOR EVERY KILOGRAM OF FOOD WE EAT, 10 KG OF WASTE ARE GENERATED ALONG THE FOOD CHAIN.
FOR CONSUMER GOODS THE TRAIL OF WASTE CAN BE MUCH GREATER.

FOOD IS SHARING

Aminata D. Traoré
Malia, writer and one of the founders of the African Social Forum
Photo Marilaide Ghigliano

GLOBAL/LOCAL

And so ever-growing numbers of human beings now do not have enough food. Getting enough to eat becomes a real feat, even one of the greatest worries for the children of the Earth, which is still always generous.

With absurd irony, hunger is above all the lot of small-scale producers (farmers, herders, fisherfolk) who pay a heavy tribute to commercial globalization. This tends to concentrate the immense riches of the Earth in an increasingly polarized way, in the hands of a privileged minority. Those who are hungry are therefore starved. Those who die of hunger are murdered, as pointed out by Jean Ziegler, the United Nations Special Rapporteur on the Right to Food.

Will our voices, including the voice of Slow Food, finally be heard? We hope so. Sometimes crises serve as jolts for lucidity. Because this is the case, let's put on the table the considerable quantity of skills, know-how, products, flavors and fragrances that make up the salt of the Earth and the leavening of cultures and life.

Here in Mali, we say that the true name for food is *sharing*, and we continue to be sure of this. In becoming globalized, hunger has just reminded the supporters of commercial globalization, deaf in the face of the urgent need for redistribution and social justice, that they are leading humanity to ruin.

Perhaps the time has come to reciprocally and genuinely respect and listen to each other. It is the task of all those who throughout the world are fighting for everyone's right to have enough healthy food to persevere in their noble struggle.

RURAL POOR

Tewolde Berhan Gebre Egziabher
Ethiopia, scientist and biologist of the national environment protection agency
Photos Marilaide Ghigliano

GLOBAL/LOCAL

The rural poor meet their livelihood needs by using the renewable natural resources, mostly biological, that their immediate environment can provide. Understandably, therefore, their impact on their immediate ecosystems is intense. Conversely, their knowledge of it is intimate.

Globalization is increasingly intensifying their impact by changing population dynamics, by superimposing global demands upon their local demands, and even by modifying the environmental factors that had hitherto maintained their ecosystem, especially climate.

INVISIBLE

Abject poverty is unbearable whether it is urban or rural. Therefore, the poor should not attract greater attention simply because they are rural. However, the rural poor are subject to more unpredictability of their meager income than are the urban poor. They are mostly crop cultivators with or without rearing animals. Some of them are entirely pastoralists. Their produce is subject to seasonal, annual and periodic vagaries of the weather, pests and diseases. On the whole, they cannot even store food produced in good years for use in bad years—they are technologically handicapped. Neither can they transport food from areas of surplus production to areas of scarcity—they are infrastructurally handicapped. Nor can they buy food from the market once their own agriculture fails them—they are financially handicapped. Therefore, they are not as robust as their average annual production and community life of mutual support suggest, but as vulnerable as their lowest annual production dictates. Their governments are usually run by the urban elite who have little understanding of these problems. This is largely because the members of the elite usually merely mimic urban-centered western governance systems, which they studied at school and which are now lauded and promoted by the international laws and norms of globalization with its contrasting individualistic values. Any community initiative that the rural poor could take to overcome their weaknesses as individuals is thus undermined and they remain insignificant, even though they constitute the majority in their respective countries. They are thus forced to try to satisfy individually their present needs at the expense of the ecosystem's ability to meet those needs also in the future.

VICIOUS CIRCLE

Consequently, de-vegetation results because wood is burnt for fuel or used for other purposes, and grass is overgrazed by domestic animals. Biodiversity is decimated. Farms loose their fertility because the nutrients removed with the harvested crops are not compensated for through manuring, fallowing or even crop rotation. The soil is eroded by water and wind. The hydrological cycle is disrupted. Floods after rains and desiccation in the dry season become common. The land gets degraded. The whole process is accelerated by climate change which is, itself, exacerbated by the very process of land degradation. The people get trapped in an environmental vicious cycle.

The urban-centered wealthy part of the world usually pours money and grain to help save lives when famines strike the rural poor. But the relief does not last long enough to break the vicious cycle. The technological, infrastructural and governance handicaps remain entrenched. Therefore, famines keep recurring at quicker intervals, breeding dependency. Aid thus fails to help the rural poor help themselves.

WEAK SYSTEMS

Nevertheless, the rural poor continue to be prey to the globalizing individualistic urban rich who prescribe 'Free Trade' as a panacea for all ills. Trade indeed improves life when there is enough production to trade with, and when it is transacted among equals and thus becomes genuinely free. Instead, the disabled agricultural systems of the rural poor are pitted in competition against the highly subsidized agriculture of the industrialized world. That is why the Agreement on Agriculture of the World Trade Organization (WTO) has been so contentious. It looks as if it will no longer be contentious since food prices are rising globally.

Even the discontinuation of agricultural subsidies, though good, would not suffice. The Agreement on Trade-related Aspects of Intellectual Property Rights (TRIPs) of the WTO is being used to rob the rural poor of their biodiversity and traditional knowledge. These rural community innovations are being privatized by rich companies and patented or protected by breeders' rights. Genetic engineering of crops has now made these patents contagious. Cross-pollination introduces patented genes from fields of genetically-engineered varieties to the fields planted with the rural poor's own non-genetically engineered varieties. Article 34 of TRIPs thus makes the rural poor infringers, as if the contamination of their genetic resources were not unjust enough.[1]

It could be possible to turn globalization into a liberating force for the rural poor. But that would require global re-orientation. Article 8(j) of the Convention on Biological Diversity[2] could be used to start a new global process to makie the rural indigenous and local communities benefit from their own innovations. Rural people would then augment their intimate knowledge of the land with the financial capacity to apply that knowledge to heal the Earth. The healing Earth would then absorb more carbon. More and more

food would also be produced where it is to be consumed. Carbon emission would then decrease and the diversity and quality of food would grow. Humanity would then strengthen rather than disrupt natural processes. Humanity's future would then be assured.

Notes
1. Article 34 Process Patents: Burden of Proof
1) For the purposes of civil proceedings in respect of the infringement of the rights of the owner referred to in paragraph 1(b) of Article 28, if the subject matter of a patent is a process for obtaining a product, the judicial authorities shall have the authority to order the defendant to prove that the process to obtain an identical product is different from the patented process. Therefore, Members shall provide, in at least one of the following circumstances, that any identical product when produced without the consent of the patent owner shall, in the absence of proof to the contrary, be deemed to have been obtained by the patented process: (a) if the product obtained by the patented process is new; (b) if there is a sub-

stantial likelihood that the identical product was made by the process and the owner of the patent has been unable through reasonable efforts to determine the process actually used.
2) Any Member shall be free to provide that the burden of proof indicated in paragraph 1 shall be on the alleged infringer only if the condition referred to in subparagraph (a) is fulfilled or only if the condition referred to in subparagraph (b) is fulfilled.
3) In the adduction of proof to the contrary, the legitimate interests of defendants in protecting their manufacturing and business secrets shall be taken into account.
2. Each Contracting Party shall, as far as possible and as appropriate [...] Subject to its national legislation, respect, preserve and maintain knowledge, innovations and practices of indigenous and local communities embodying traditional lifestyles relevant for the conservation and sustainable use of biological diversity and promote their wider application with the approval and involvement of the holders of such knowledge, innovations and practices and encourage the equitable sharing of the benefits arising from the utilization of such knowledge, innovations and practices.

Slow Food membership

Membership growth internationally

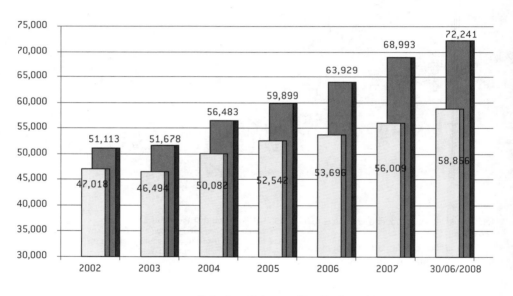

☐ National associations   ■ Slow Food members

On 30/06/2008 Slow Food had 72,241 active members. Membership has grown sizably over the years. It is important to point out that, if in 2002 92 percent of members belonged to the national associations in Italy, USA, Germany, Switzerland, United Kingdom, Japan and France), by June 2008 the percentage had dropped to 81, the number of members in the rest of the world having increased.

Membership by geographical areas

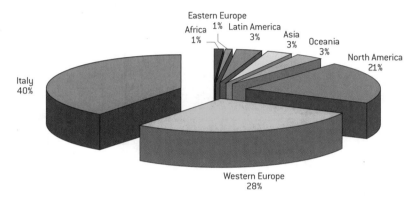

Membership growth in developing countries

The most significant increase in membership in developing countries came in the wake of Terra Madre 2006. During the 'meeting of food communities', over 600 delegates from such countries decided to join. From 2002 to 2006 the number of members from these countries rose from 1.5 percent to almost 6 percent of the total. In 2006 the number increased by 94 percent, in 2007 by 73 percent.

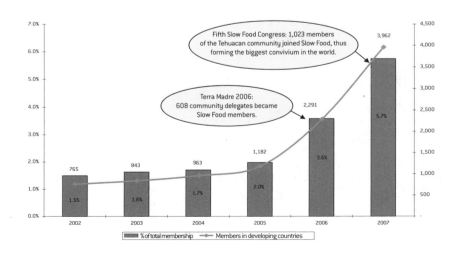

Countries with more than 1,000 members

Countries with more than 1,000 members. In four years, the number has doubled.

2003

2007

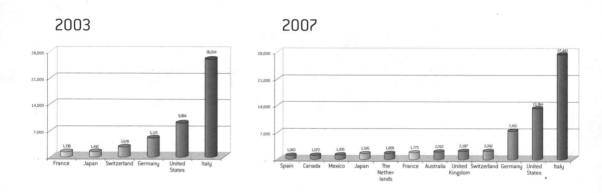

Slow Food worldwide

Slow Food convivia

88 countries
1167 convivia

Slow Food members

132 countries

Terra Madre and Slow Food

150 countries

(Data at August 2008)

Terra Madre

Participants by geographical origin

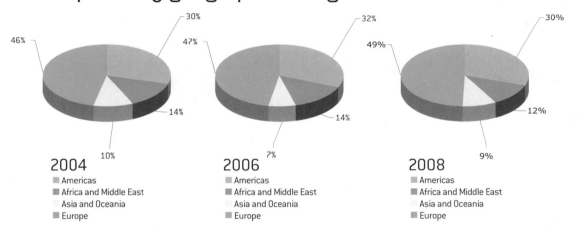

2004
- Americas
- Africa and Middle East
- Asia and Oceania
- Europe

2006
- Americas
- Africa and Middle East
- Asia and Oceania
- Europe

2008
- Americas
- Africa and Middle East
- Asia and Oceania
- Europe

Participants by category

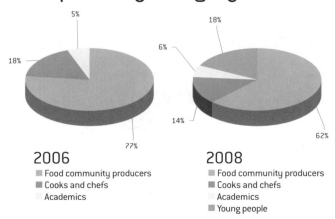

2006
- Food community producers
- Cooks and chefs
- Academics

2008
- Food community producers
- Cooks and chefs
- Academics
- Young people

Taste education worldwide

(Data at June 2008)

Afghanistan
Community of Herat raisin producers – Activities involving students at the University of Herat

Argentina
Mar Del Plata Convivium – Educational activities

Armenia
Community of cereal producers – School garden

Australia
Central Victoria Convivium – 'Spudhunters', potato education activity for children
Perth Convivium – School garden
Adelaide Hills Convivium – School garden
Saddleback Convivium – Workshops

Austria
Voralberg Convivium – Mini Cooks
Wien Convivium – Food culture activities for refugee children
Styria Convivium – 16 school garden projects
Wachau Plus Convivium – Dairy workshops

Belgium
Les saveurs de Silly Convivium – School Garden
Liège Convivium – Canteen catering

Belarus
Briosa Convivium – Sensory education for children

Brazil
Rio de Janeiro Convivium and Terra Madre cook – Cooking with manioc in local schools
Brasilia Convivium and Terra Madre volunteers – Educational activities

Bulgaria
Community of Karakachan Nomadic Breeders – Educational activities at a traditional research center

Canada
Cape Breton Convivium – School Garden
Manitoba Convivium – Taste workshops for women producers
Perth County Convivium – Taste education TV program for colleges
Terra Madre Project, Nova Scotia – Taste education classes in schools, School garden
Ste Sault Marie Convivium – Cooking classes for school children
Vancouver Convivium – University farm and sensory workshops
Vancouver Island Convivium – School garden

Côte d'Ivoire
Convivium and Terra Madre communities – School canteen projects

Cuba
Terra Madre Food communities food preservation projects

Democratic Republic of Congo
Kiwanja Convivium – Raising awareness on traditional foods in colleges

France
Slow Food France – Projects with agricultural colleges and catering schools , St Chaumond project with a catering school
Roussillon Convivium – School garden
Biarn Convivium – Project for immigrant children in rural areas

Georgia
Terra Madre Project – Taste education in schools

Germany
Slow Food Germany – Collaboration with Darmstadt/Alice Hospital
Slow Food Germany – Taste workshops organized at exhibitions and Slow Food events
Munich Convivium – Slow Mobil
Stuttgart Convivium – Regular activities in primary schools
Oldenburg Convivium – Kiko Cooking Club
Bremen Convivium – Three 'schoolyard' projects, including courses on food quality for teachers
Mecklenburgische Seenplatte Convivium – 'Marihn Garden' School Garden

Hong Kong
Hong Kong Convivium – Educational farms visits

India
Mumbai Convivium – Young Ecologist' program
Delhi Convivium – Good Food Program in schools

Indonesia
Jakarta Convivium – Taste workshops

Ireland
Cork and Dublin Convivium – Internships and exchanges
Dublin Convivium – School garden, Cooking classes in disadvantaged areas, Cheesemaking workshops

Israel
School and community gardens

Italy
127 convivium gardens, Master of Food courses (24 subjects), Taste Workshops, teacher training courses, School Canteens projects, classes on food education in hospitals and prisons, taste education for children during events.

Japan
Slow Food – Master of Food

Kenya
Central Rift Convivium – School gardens

Kyrgyzstan
Almaty Convivium – Classes for producers and college students

Latvia
Riga Convivium – Taste education workshops in schools with food producers, TV program to raise awareness of Slow Food activities

Macao
Macau Convivium – Raising awareness/Education of the Slow Food philosophy in colleges

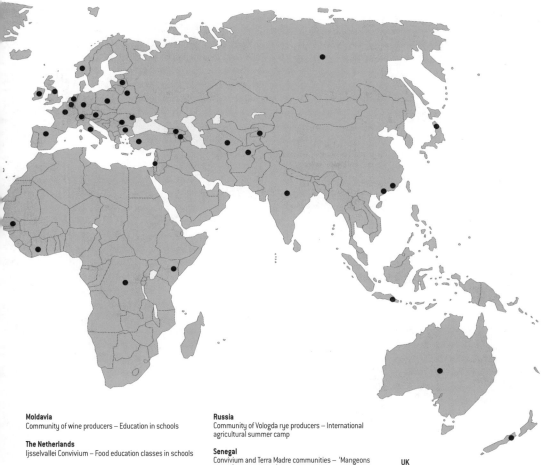

Moldavia
Community of wine producers – Education in schools

The Netherlands
Ijsselvallei Convivium – Food education classes in schools

New Zealand
Waitakere Convivium – School garden

Norway
Lofoten Convivium – Sensory workshops

Poland
Community of Opole breadmakers – Training and cooking classes on traditional cuisine
Community of organic producers – Taste workshops for students

Romania
Turda Convivium – School garden
Brusturoasa Convivium – Taste workshops

Russia
Community of Vologda rye producers – International agricultural summer camp

Senegal
Convivia and Terra Madre communities – 'Mangeons Local' (Let's Eat Local) food education project in schools

Spain
Zaragoza Convivium – Food education for students
Asturias Convivium – Taste education in hospitals
Bilbao-Bizkaia Convivium – Education space at the Alondiga and Al Gusto - Saber y Sabor fairs

Switzerland
Engadin Convivium – School garden

Turkey
Istanbul Convivium – Food education in schools

Turkmenistan
Ahal Convivium – Sensory workshops in schools

UK
Shrewsbury Convivium – School garden
Bedford Convivium – Park Wood Community orchard project
East Lothian Convivium – Locally sourced school lunches
Herefordshire Convivium –'Fabulous Food' project
Oxford University Convivium – Education on daily food

United States
Slow Food USA – 'Garden to Table' projects in 35 schools, 12 Slow Food on Campus convivial, Taste workshops

For information:
education@slowfood.com

Presidia round the world

118 projects in 45 countries
179 Italian Presidia
(at 30/08/2008)

Western Europe
Austria – Vienna Gemischter Satz Wines
Austria – Wiesenwienerwald Chequers
Cyprus – Tsamarella
France – Gascony Chicken
France – Mirandeise Nacré Cow
France –Barèges-Gavarnie Mouton
France – Bigorre Black Pig
France – Haute-Provence Einkorn
France – Pardailhan Black Turnip
France – Pélardon Affiné
France – Roussillon Rancio Sec
France – Saint-Flour Planèze Golden Lentil
Germany – Champagner Bratbirne Pear Spumante
Ireland – Irish Raw Milk Cheese
Netherlands – Aged Artisan Gouda
Netherlands – Chaam Hen
Netherlands – Oosterschelde Lobster
Netherlands – Texel Sheep Cheese
Norway – Artisan Sognefjord Geitost
Norway – Møre og Romsdal Salt Cod
Norway – Sørøya Island Stockfish
Norway – Cured and Smoked Sunnmøre Herrings
Norway – Villsau Sheep
Portugal – Mirandesa Sausage
Portugal – Serpa Cheese
Spain – Ballobar Capers
Spain – Carranzana Cara Negra Sheep Cheese
Spain – Euskal Txerria Pig
Spain – Maestrat Millenary Olive Trees Extra Virgin Oil
Spain – Ganxet Bean
Spain – Jiloca Saffron
Spain – Mungia Talo
Spain – Sitges Malvasia
Spain – Tolosa Black Bean
Sweden – Reindeer Suovas
Sweden – Jamtland Cellar-matured Goat Cheese
Switzerland – Bedretto Valley Artisan Pastries
Switzerland – Farina Bona
Switzerland – Traditional Kirsch
Switzerland – Locarno Valley Cicitt
Switzerland – Muggio Valley Zincarlin
Switzerland – Müstair Valley Rye Bread

Switzerland – Wallis Traditional Rye Bread
United Kingdom – Artisan Somerset Cheddar
United Kingdom – Fal Oyster
United Kingdom – Gloucester Cheese
United Kingdom – Old Gloucester Beef
United Kingdom – Three Counties Perry

Central and Eastern Europe
Belorus – Rosson Wild Fruits and Infusions
Bosnia and Herzegovina – Pozegaca Plum Slatko
Bosnia and Herzegovina – Sack Cheese (Sir iz Mijeha)
Bulgaria – Tcherni Vit Green Sirene Cheese
Bulgaria – Karakachan Sheep
Croatia – Giant Istrian Ox
Croatia – Ljubitovica Garlic
Georgia – Georgian Amphora Wine
Hungary – Mangalica Sausage
Poland – Oscypek Cheese
Poland – Polish Mead
Romania – Brânzá de Burduf
Romania – Saxon Village Preserves
Uzbekistan – Bostalyk Almond

Middle-East
Afghanistan – Herat Raisin
Lebanon – Darfiyeh
Lebanon – Kechek el Fouqara Cheese

North America
Canada – Red Fife Wheat
United States of America – Anishinaabeg Manoomin Rice
United States of America – Cape May Oyster
United States of America – Makah Ozette Potato
United States of America – Navajo-Churro Sheep
United States of America – Raw Milk Cheese
United States of America – Sebastopol Gravenstein Apple

Latin America
Argentina – Andean Corn
Argentina – Quebrada de Humahuaca Andean Potatoes
Argentina – Yacón
Bolivia – Pando Brazil Nut
Brazil – Aratù

Brazil – Barù Nut
Brazil – Canapù Bean
Brazil – Juçara Palm Heart
Brazil – Red Rice
Brazil – Sateré Mawé Canudo Bee Honey
Brazil – Sateré Mawé Native Waranà
Brazil – Serra Catarinense Pine Nuts
Brazil – Umbù
Chile – Blue Egg Hen
Chile – Calbuco Black-Bordered Oyster
Chile – Merquèn
Chile – Purén White Strawberries

Chile – Robinson Crusoe Island Seafood
Dominican Republic – Sierra Cafetalera Coffee
Ecuador – Cacao Nacional
Guatemala – Huehuetenango Highlands Coffee
Guatemala – Ixcán Cardamom
Mexico – Chinantla Vanilla
Mexico – Seri Indians Roasted Mesquite
Mexico – Tehuacán Amaranth
Peru – San Marcos Andean Fruit
Peru – Pampacorral Sweet Potatoes
Peru – Andean Kañihua
Peru – Traditional White Chuño

Africa
Cape Verde – Bolona Plateau Goat Cheese
Egypt – Siwa Dates
Ethiopia – Wenchi Volcano Honey
Ethiopia – Wukro White Honey
Ethiopia – Harenna Forest Wild Coffee
Madagascar – Andasibe Red Rice
Madagascar – Mananara Vanilla
Mali – Dogon Somè
Morocco – Argan Oil
Morocco – Taliouine Saffron
Mauritania – Imraguen Women's Mullet Bottarga

Asia
Armenia – Motal
China – Tibetan Plateau Yak Cheese
India – Dehra Dun Basmati Rice
Japan – Unzen Green Mustard
Malaysia – Bario Rice
Malaysia – Rimbàs Black Pepper

For information:
www.fondazioneslowfood.com

Slow Food Financial Statement 2007

In 2007 Slow Food worked on a budget of about 2,420,000 euros. With respect to the past when resources utilized were slightly in excess of 2 million euros, the 2007 budget comprised the 400,000 euros necessary to organize the 5th International Congress.

Proceeds from membership fees	959,804
Contributions for event organization	103,060
Contributions for projects and donations	299,874
Contributions for the Terra Madre community network	882,000
Contribution from International Congress delegates	172,720
Total Slow Food revenue	**2,417,458**
Membership development activities	245,206
Communication	280,889
Contributions to developing countries	221,359
Other projects	118,544
Labor costs	749,162
Structural costs	254,681
Tied-up reserve provision	150,000
International Congress	385,666
Total Slow Food expenditure	**2,405,507**
Operating result	**11,951**

Breakdown of Slow Food funding (2007)

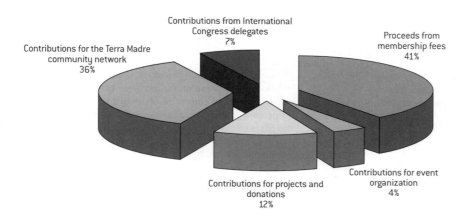

Contributions from International Congress delegates
7%

Contributions for the Terra Madre community network
36%

Proceeds from membership fees
41%

Contributions for projects and donations
12%

Contributions for event organization
4%

Membership fees were Slow Food's main source of funding (41 percent). International events (Slow Fish in Genoa, Cheese in Bra and Algusto, Saber y Sabor in Bilbao) generated 4 percent of proceeds; donations and contributions for projects from foundations, associations and individual supporters accounted for 12 percent. Contributions for the Terra Madre network (36 percent) were allocated to cover the costs incurred to coordinate and develop the food community network. The contribution made by international delegates from developed countries to cover part of the costs of the Fifth International Congress accounted for 7 percent.

Breakdown of Slow Food costs (2007)

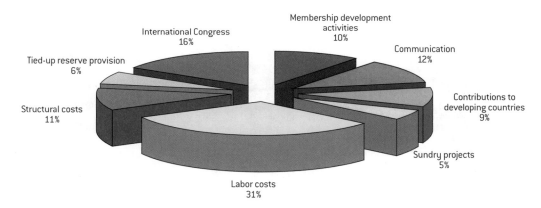

International Congress
16%

Tied-up reserve provision
6%

Structural costs
11%

Membership development
activities
10%

Communication
12%

Contributions to
developing countries
9%

Sundry projects
5%

Labor costs
31%

In 2007 membership development activities (10 percent of resources) comprised member service, travel and accommodation expenses. Communication—the publication of the Slow international journal (replaced by the Slow Food Almanac in 2008) and national newsletters, and advocacy activities for the promulgation of the movement—accounted for 12 percent of resources through. Contributions to developing countries accounted for 9 percent of investment in 2007. The beneficiaries of these provisions were presidium producers in developing countries and Terra Madre food communities in Africa and Latin America. The 'Sundry projects' entry (5 percent) comprised a mass media awareness campaign on sustainability issues and the costs of participation in international events. Human resources were the highest cost item (31 percent) for the coordination of membership and Terra Madre community development. Structural costs (11 percent) refer to rentals and overheads, data processing and telephone systems, administration and bank expenses, and taxes. 6 percent of resources was allocated to ensure the capitalization of the international association. The Fifth International Congress in Puebla, finally, absorbed 16 percent of resources.

The Slow Food Foundation for Biodiversity

The Slow Food Foundation for Biodiversity supports Presidium and Earth Market producer communities. The 2007 budget amounted to about 1,129,000 euros of which 88 percent were redistributed among the Foundation's various stakeholders (net Added Value), or producers (Ark of Taste, Presidia, Earth Markets and other projects), the local communities, involved in and sensitized through communication activities on issues relating to the defense of biodiversity and Foundation personnel.

Financial Statement 2007

Proceeds from supporters	477,964
Contributions from the Slow Food world	223,393
Events	146,889
Proceeds from projects	147,156
Sundry proceeds	133,324
Total Slow Food revenue	**1,128,726**
Presidium projects	398,217
Earth Markets	53,768
Cooperation projects	99,131
Communication and community sensitization	105,756
Labor costs	336,517
Structural costs	135,337
Total Slow Food expenditure	**1,128,726**
Operating result	**—**

Breakdown of distributed added value 2007

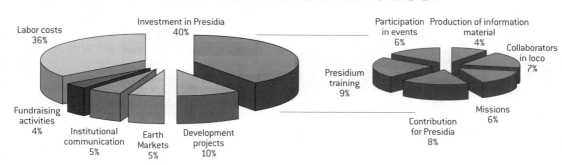

Labor costs 36%
Investment in Presidia 40%
Participation in events 6%
Production of information material 4%
Collaborators in loco 7%
Presidium training 9%
Fundraising activities 4%
Institutional communication 5%
Earth Markets 5%
Development projects 10%
Contribution for Presidia 8%
Missions 6%

Terra Madre Foundation

The network of food communities is managed by the Terra Madre Foundation, the founding members of which are Slow Food, the Italian Ministry of Foreign Affairs – Cooperation for Development, the Italian Ministry of Agricultural, Food and Forestry Policies, the Piedmont Regional Authority and the City of Turin. Together these bodies collected about 6,600,000 euros in the two-year period 2006/07. In 2006 the Terra Madre world meeting constituted the main cost item, comprising organization and staging expenses as well as the travel and accommodation costs of the delegates of the various food communities and, in 2007, the year after the meeting, the expenses incurred, mainly labor costs, to maintain and develop the network. This statement does not take into account the activities developed by the network in loco in the different countries.

Terra Madre Financial Statement 2006/2007

Contributions collected to support the communities	6,622,963
Total Terra Madre Foundation revenue	6,622,963
Terra Madre event cost	1,624,118
Community travel expenses	1,760,841
Community hospitality expenses	690,475
Institutional communication	224,399
Labor costs	1,738,872
Structural costs	559,753
Total Slow Food costs	6,598,458
Operating result	24,505

Breakdown of spending 2006/2007

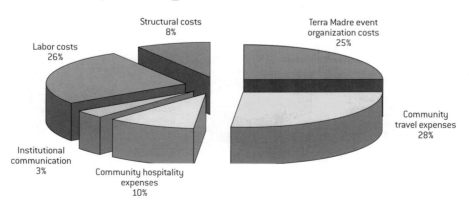

Structural costs
8%

Terra Madre event
organization costs
25%

Labor costs
26%

Institutional
communication
3%

Community hospitality
expenses
10%

Community
travel expenses
28%

Organization

The Slow Food international movement is coordinated by an International Board of Directors and guided by an International Council. Appointments have a duration of four years. The main headquarters of Slow Food International is in Bra in Piedmont, Italy. In some countries—Italy, USA, Germany, Switzerland, France, Japan, UK, Australia, The Netherlands—activities are run by National Managements, which respond to the International Board of Directors.

International Board of Directors

President
Carlo Petrini (Italy)

Vice-Presidents
Alice Waters (USA)
Vandana Shiva (India)
John Kariuki Mwangi (Kenya)

Secretary
Paolo Di Croce (Italy)

Members
Roberto Burdese (Italy)
Allen Katz (USA)
Otto Geisel (Germany)
Silvija Davidson (UK)
Rafael Pérez (Switzerland)
Jean Lhéritier (France)
Hirotoshi Wako (Japan)

INTERNATIONAL COUNCIL *

Italy
Roberto Burdese
Silvio Barbero
Massimo Bernacchini
Marco Brogiotti
Daniele Buttignol
Valeria Cometti
Antonello Del Vecchio
Andrea Pezzana

USA
Allen Katz
Erika Lesser
Jeff Roberts
Peter De Garmo
Joel Smith

Germany
Otto Geisel
Walter Kress
Lars Jäger
Silke Schneider

UK
Silvija Davidson
Ian Pratt
John Fleming

Switzerland
Rafael Pérez
Giorgio Romano
Markus Gehri

France
Jean Lhéritier
Lucien Biolatto

Japan
Hirotoshi Wako
Yutaka Kayaba

Australia
Leonie Furber
Ann Shaw Rungie

Austria
Manfred Flieser

Brazil
Roberta Marins de Sá

Bulgaria
Dessislava Dimitrova

Canada
Sinclair Philip

Ireland
Darina Allen

Kenya
Samuel Karanja Muhunyu

Mexico
Raúl Hernández Garciadiego

The Netherlands
Jan Wolf
Geert Veenendaal

Spain
Mariano Gómez Fernández

Sweden
Ola Buckard

Slow Food Foundation for Biodiversity Representative
Serena Milano (Italy)

University of Gastronomic Sciences Representative
Cinzia Scaffidi (Italy)

* All members of the International Board of Directors are also members of the International Council. All members of the International Council were elected for a four-year term of office during the Slow Food International Congress in Puebla, Mexico, 2007.